GRASSROOTS DEMOCRACY

Local Government in the Maritimes

Kell Antoft and Jack Novack

Henson College, Dalhousie University

Canadian Cataloguing in Publication Data

Antoft, Kell, 1923 –

Grassroots government

Includes bibliographical references and index.
ISBN 0-7703-1014-1

1. Municipal government -- Maritime Provinces. 2. Local government -- Maritime Provinces. I. Novack, Jack, 1951 – II. Title

JS1721.M34A68 1998 352.14'09715 C98-950211-2

Published by Henson College, Dalhousie University
6100 University Avenue
Halifax, Nova Scotia
B3H 3J5

Design: GaynorSarty, Halifax
Printed: Atlantic Nova Print, Halfax, Nova Scotia

This book is dedicated to the late

Professor Lothar Richter and
Dr. Guy Henson, O.C.

Maritime pioneers in the reinforcement
of grassroots democracy through
research and education.

Preface

Dalhousie, in 1936, became one of the first Canadian universities to recognize the educational needs of the local level of government. In that year, at the conclusion of the annual conference of the Union of Nova Scotia Municipalities (UNSM), Professor Lothar Richter, the first Director of the Institute of Public Affairs, initiated the first of what was to become a series of seminars for municipal clerks. This event marked the beginning of university-based continuing education for municipal administrators in the Maritime provinces and led to acceptance of local government as a field of academic research and consultation. Professor Richter's efforts to build on the co-operation between the UNSM and the Institute was a key factor in this initial success.

After Guy Henson's appointment, in 1956, as Director of the Institute of Public Affairs, the Municipal Administration Program became a centrepiece of the Institute's activities. A wide array of educational programs were developed, including seminars, conferences, and correspondence courses. Participants in these activities involved both elected and administrative municipal officials, including assessors, planners, education administrators, and police and fire protection officers. Most of the programs were directed towards the interests and needs of local governments in the Maritime provinces, but over the years, increasing numbers of students from elsewhere in Canada have become involved.

Parallel with its educational activities, the Municipal Administration Program also became an advisory resource on municipal issues in the Atlantic provinces. The focus on local government studies helped to attract academic interest to the field and led to new opportunities for research. An indirect result of this interest has been the Dalhousie School of Public Administration's development of several municipal administration activities with the school.

After the merger, in 1986, of the Institute of Public Affairs with the Dalhousie Office of Part-Time Studies and Continuing Education to form Henson College, the section dealing with municipal matters has continued in development and offering of courses and consultancy. As elsewhere in university life, budgetary considerations have often curtailed the urge to innovate and create, but Henson College has been able to maintain its eminent position as a Canadian centre for research and education in local government.

The present volume was conceived as a special contribution to mark the 60th anniversary of Richter's launch of the first continuing education event for municipal officials in the Maritimes. The huge changes being experienced by local governments in the mid-1990's, however, made it difficult to forecast whether a text dealing with the present state of local government in the Maritimes would remain relevant for any significant period of time. Only in the past year or so has the pace of change seemed to moderate, but we must still issue a caution that descriptions herein are only a snapshot of the situation as it existed at the time of writing.

A word is necessary to explain the origins and motivation for this *Grassroots Democracy* volume. In 1977, the Institute of Public Affairs published the first edition of *A Guide to Local Government in Nova Scotia*. Second and third editions followed in 1984 and 1992 respectively. These editions were written primarily for use by municipal councillors or citizens considering offering for election. Successive printings gained an increasingly broad audience among academic colleagues, students, and members of the general public. This acceptance suggested that a work with a broader Maritime appeal would be useful, especially if it dealt less with technical details and included issues that are of general interest to citizens in any community in the region.

The text in this volume is intended not only as a guide to the development of local government and how it operates but it also seeks to identify the principal political issues that have brought local government to its present state. Readers will notice that the authors have a strong bias towards local government as the cornerstone of our democratic traditions and ideals. We have not sought to avoid sensitive issues or to paper over tensions that may occur in relations between the provincial and local levels. These are matters that need to be understood and explored in order to fully appreciate the importance of local government to the future of our region and our county. We lament the complacency that is reflected by the low voter turnout in most municipal elections as well as in the empty spectator seats at council meetings, but we interpret this as the need for more informed discussion of why local governments really matter.

For those readers who tackle the book from cover to cover, the occurrence of repetitive facts, ideas, and explanations from one chapter to another may seem irritating. Our experience suggests, however, that many readers will approach *Grassroots Democracy* as a reference book rather than as recreational reading. For that reason, we have attempted to provide sufficient background for each topic so that individual chapters may be read without continually referring backwards or forwards to other sections of the book.

The elimination of detailed references to specific legislation or regulations is intended to minimize the listing of endless differences among the three provinces, but will hopefully also make the text more appealing to a wider range of readership. For those who may wish to explore particular subjects, Appendix A contains a list of suggested additional sources and readings. Appendix B carries a listing of the principal legislative Acts applicable in each province.

The writing of this book has been longer and more complex than originally planned. But generous aid and advice from public officials at the provincial and municipal levels and from academic colleagues has made the work highly satisfying. We especially wish to acknowledge two individuals who reviewed the manuscripts in draft form and provided helpful comments. They are Charles S. Shannon, Consultant and former Municipal Manager and Municipal Solicitor, and Dennis Friesen, former Director of Community Planning, Prince Edward Island Department of Provincial Affairs and Attorney General. Additionally, we wish to thank Debbie Kampen and Sherry Carmont-MacBean for their careful copy editing.

Kell Antoft
Jack Novack

Contents

Chapter I: Historical Overview: Local Government in the Maritime Provinces

Chapter II: Local Government in the Scheme of Things

Chapter III: Local Government and the Law

Chapter IV: What Does Local Government Do?

Chapter V: Municipal Decision Making

Chapter VI: Public Participation

Chapter VII: Municipal Finance

Chapter VIII: Planning in the Community

Chapter IX: Operations and Procedures of Municipal Council

Chapter X: Offering for Service on Council

Chapter XI: After Thoughts

Chapter I

Historical Overview: Local Government in the Maritime Provinces

Introduction

To help us in our exploration of the role that municipal institutions continue to play in the fabric of our society, we will, in this chapter, review the historical roots of local government in the Maritime provinces.

We often assume that Canadian history began only when the Europeans first set foot on the North American continent. But it is worth taking note of the importance that Canada's first peoples attach to the concept of local self-government. Such dedication undoubtedly is rooted in the tribal traditions that predate the arrival of these alien visitors from across the oceans. In the early days of colonialism, however, democracy was a totally incomprehensible concept for the European newcomers.

The 1992 discussions of proposed constitutional amendments included the topic of "inherent rights" to self-government for the First Nations of Canada. These talks revealed the deep-seated traditions of shared decision-making in aboriginal communities and the hunger for a voice in all matters that affect their future. The demands were not for seats in the House of Commons or in provincial legislatures; rather the aspirations were for a system of "local" government that would enable the native populations to maintain and develop their own sense of community and culture. For readers who are interested in this subject, the 1997 Report of the Royal Commission on Aboriginal Peoples deals extensively with this issue.[1]

The colonial administrative systems that were introduced to North America in the seventeenth century took little heed of the customs of the native peoples. The policies of the European newcomers were focussed on maximizing returns from the fur trade, recruiting aboriginal warriors to assist in the continuous wars between the competing European monarchies, moving aboriginal habitations far away from land to be cul-

1 Royal Commission on Aboriginal Peoples, *Report*. Ottawa: Queen's Printer, 1997.

tivated by new settlers, and, in the process, doing their utmost to suppress the cultures and traditional religious beliefs of the "pagans". Accordingly the struggles for democracy in Canadian society have followed a path that did not benefit from lessons that we might have learned from the original inhabitants.

A Cradle of Responsible Government

In the Maritime provinces, municipal government was deeply involved in the successful struggle for responsible government, an early step on the path towards our present form of Canadian political democracy. Thus the creation of the City of Saint John, New Brunswick, was a major milestone in the evolution of local government in British North America. It occurred in 1785 as a result of demands by the 14,000 "United Empire Loyalists" who had fled to Canada during and immediately after the American Revolution and had settled on lands at the mouth of the Saint John River. As refugees, they were in dire need of many essentials, including the organization of policing, fire protection, and other kinds of community services. They petitioned the colonial Lieutenant-Governor to create a local government to organize such services. The outcome was the royal charter of incorporation of Saint John as a city, the first municipality in the British North American colonies that were later to become Canada.

The special needs of Saint John grew out of the sudden influx of a large mass of uprooted people into a small area. Elsewhere in the Maritime provinces, population growth was more gradual and, with only a few exceptions, was mainly dispersed in more rural settlements. Here the main form of local administration was the colonial system of Courts of Quarter Sessions, dispensing local justice and providing for elementary service needs. These bodies were made up of groups of Justices of the Peace for each county. Besides hearing legal cases, the Justices administered whatever local services were to be provided. The appointees were generally chosen from wealthy landowners, merchants and lawyers friendly to the colonial Lieutenant-Governors. The Justices at each Session had an advisory group called the Grand Jury. This body was composed of lesser appointees drawn from the local community, but it had no say beyond its advisory opinions. Democracy was obviously not a feature of this system.

The Courts of Sessions system was to endure for many more years after Saint John became the first municipal unit in the colonies of British North America. Indeed more than half a century was to elapse before further such incorporations took place in the Maritimes.

As may be expected, the pressure for local self-rule is more likely to first appear in the larger urban settlements. This was true in Nova Scotia where the struggle for responsible government was closely linked to conflicts over the local administration of affairs in the City of Halifax. It was in this confrontation that Joseph Howe emerged as a fierce critic of the Lieutenant-Governor's inner circle. He had been brought to trial in 1835 on a charge of criminal libel following publication in his newspaper, The Nova Scotian, of a letter to the editor, alleging that officials of the Halifax Court of Sessions were guilty of fraud, embezzlement and abuse of power. In the famous court proceedings, Howe, speaking in his own defence, vigorously criticized these officials and their lack of accountability to the citizens of Halifax. Howe emerged triumphant and shortly after ran successfully for a seat in the House of Assembly. His actions not only laid the foundation for freedom of the press in Nova Scotia, but also helped to ignite the successful struggle for responsible and more democratic local government. His campaign made possible the incorporation, in 1841, of the City of Halifax, six years after the trial

At the time of Confederation, the region had only a few incorporated municipalities with elected councils. In New Brunswick there were the cities of Saint John and Fredericton, two towns and three county units. Nova Scotia had only the City of Halifax. Prince Edward Island had the City of Charlottetown.

Municipal government had thus come to the urban centres first, with the smaller towns and rural areas not following until well after Confederation. For example, county local governments became general in New Brunswick and Nova Scotia only with mandatory legislation in 1877 and 1879 respectively, in both cases with less than enthusiastic support from most residents. In PEI, the Legislative Assembly enacted the Town Act in 1870 to allow communities to incorporate, but the Town of Summerside was the only community to apply before the turn of the century.

Provincial governments earlier had shown reluctance in allowing local self-government, but by the late 1870's they had undergone a change of heart. The reason for this change was simple: municipal governments were now seen as a way for provincial governments to shift some of their rising costs, particularly for road and bridge construction, onto the local property tax base. Thus the idea of downloading is not a recent phenomenon!

The mandatory creation of rural municipalities in New Brunswick and Nova Scotia finally aroused requests for town incorporations by more populated urban communities. Impatient with the minimal services and lack of accountability of the Courts of Sessions and Grand Juries, public pressure brought about a number of town incorporations and led to the adoption, in both provinces, of the general bills to standardize and facilitate the incorporation process.

Impact of Technology

The period around the turn of the century brought a number of significant changes for society, which have had their impact on our own as well as on other municipal governments throughout the world. These revolved around technological changes, two of the most dramatic being the introduction of electrical power, and the replacement of horse transportation by the automobile and other transport vehicles. The new energy source made an enormous change in work conditions. For municipal governments, it made street lighting an entirely new and different service, it provided power that made decentralized industrial location possible, it introduced rapid urban transit as a major service challenge, and for many municipalities it gave new meaning to the whole question of utility management. For transportation, the automobile created vastly different demands in road construction and maintenance, it added traffic control to policing functions, and it had radical implications for location of both residential and commercial developments. Over time the automobile created suburbs, shopping centres and industrial parks, made the need for backyard barns and carriage houses obsolete, and brought in new issues of air pollution, parking facilities, and urban core decline. A huge proportion of the work force formerly occupied in caring for horses, building and driving of horse drawn carriages, manufacturing and repairing of harness, growing and distribution of oats, and sweeping up of droppings, were all rather abruptly transferred to the ranks of the unemployed. As we travel further into the century, the changes multiply from these and other innovations, as do the challenges to our ability to adapt.

In the Maritime provinces, the advent of steam and iron ships made sail and wooden ships obsolete for all but the fishery. The shipbuilding industry, which had provided substantial economic momentum to the regional economy, was literally wiped out over a few decades. With it went a substantial part of the export trade in lumber products as well as the return cargoes from the erstwhile markets in Europe and the Carribean. This setback is often cited as a crucial watershed for the economy of the Maritime provinces.

The Period of World Wars

The first World War of 1914-18 brought major upheaval in the affairs and lives of Maritimers, as it did for all Canadians. In Halifax, the 1917 disaster of the Great Explosion created chaos that placed immense challenges on the municipality for many years to come. Throughout the Maritime provinces, the war's aftermath and the economic and social shifts that arrived with the returning veterans changed the complexion of rural society and hastened the pace and problems of urbanization.

Crisis followed crisis. The Great Depression of the thirties was particularly devastating for the Maritime provinces. The collapse of much of the already fragile secondary industry in the region caused severe hardship across the whole spectrum of society. The growing burden of unemployment relief drained municipal resources and placed a number of units in precarious financial situations.

World War II and its aftermath brought a new set of changes that differed markedly from those after the first World War. First of all, conditions for the new crop of veterans was vastly more hopeful. Programs for resettlement included assistance for housing, generous allowances for educational programs both at the secondary and post-secondary levels, and provision of comprehensive medical and emotional support services for the special needs arising from the trauma and stresses of war.

On the broader front, the vision of a society that offered greater social security for all its members was epitomized by the catch phrase: "care from cradle to the grave", a motto that had been coined in the United Kingdom by Sir William Beveridge. His *Beveridge Report*, the blueprint for social security and the welfare state in Britain, became the inspiration for a similar approach in Canada. Unemployment insurance and family allowances were important milestones towards the creation of the Canadian model.

Welfare and social services had been a traditional responsibility of charities and local authorities in all of the Canadian provinces. The old Poor Law was the forerunner of the range of services that came under local administration over time. As our social responsibility ethos evolved, communities were expected to keep pace with the escalating needs of those sidelined by a rapidly urbanizing society. Rowat, writing in 1954, described some of these challenges:

> It is well known that parts of many towns and cities are unsightly and noisy, are crowded and are jerry-built, and contain slums that are breeding grounds for disease, crime and child delin-

quency. Adult education, public libraries, public concerts and plays, parks and playgrounds, auditoriums, swimming-pools and rinks, traffic police for schools, juvenile courts, day-nurseries, health clinics, housing and slum clearance - all these things and many more are becoming the concern of Councils who wish to improve the cultural, recreational and social environment of their citizens.[2]

Social service issues were of course only one area of growing concern and expense for municipalities. Education costs belonged to the major expenditure sector that was increasing at the most dramatic rate, but there were others. In Nova Scotia, the provincial government adopted a pragmatic approach to resulting problems. Premier Stanfield made this explicit in the Throne Speech in 1966:

> It is the policy of my Government in relation to our municipalities to increase the Province's share of the costs of education, public health, public welfare and the administration of justice. In important instances my Government has assumed full cost, but generally some degree of local administrative and financial participation in programs in these fields is considered desirable, with the financial contribution of municipalities being related to their respective abilities to pay when such contributions are likely to affect local tax rates substantially.[3]

The Impact of Societal Change

We have touched on some of the technological changes that have posed massive challenges for Canadian society. In the Maritimes, some things have changed rapidly, but in other ways the region has lagged behind other parts of Canada. We will briefly touch on some aspects that are significant for municipal government in the three provinces.

Today the population of the region has more than doubled since Canada's first census in 1871. The rural population is about the same as a hundred years ago, although most are no longer working at farming. The number of people living in urban or suburban areas, however, has increased about seven times. The size and make-up of families has altered, the population has aged, the number of single-parent families is

2 Donald C. Rowat. *Your Local Government*. Toronto: MacMillan Co. Of Canada. 1955, p.67.
3 Cited in: J. Murray Beck. *The Evolution of Municipal Government in Nova Scotia.* Halifax: Queen's Printer, 1973, p.37.

increasing, and the proportion of people living alone has risen dramatically. The cultural mix of our population has become increasingly diversified. All of these changes pose challenges to the ability of local governments to provide a greatly expanded range of services while maintaining their role as mediators.

Communication between one part of a province and another is a great deal easier and faster than in the last century. As already noted, the automobile has been a major factor in technological change, but it has also had an immense societal effect. It has provided a degree of mobility that was unimaginable just a few generations ago, thereby radically altering the shape and size of urban communities as well as the lives of people who grew up as the automobile made its dramatic entry.

The economy of the Maritime provinces has changed, not always for the better. A century ago lumbering, shipbuilding, fishing, and agriculture were the main sources of employment. Large-scale manufacturing was unknown and in the late nineteen hundreds, only about 25,000 people were employed in various secondary industries; among them, sawmills, boot and shoe manufacturing, blacksmith establishments, shipyards, tailoring, coopering, tanneries, carpentry and joinery.

Industry has grown and become more diversified, but the growth rate has been slower than in the central provinces of Canada. The region has been particularly vulnerable to the impact and after-shocks of depressions and recessions. At the same time, as a result of better education, media communication and opportunities for travel, Maritimers have become more sophisticated. Today they expect a variety of public services, many of them municipally provided, that bear no relation to the social needs of the 1800's. At the same time, their ability to absorb the costs of services has been seriously shaken by repeated bouts of economic downturn. But of all the side effects of these changes, the out-migration of young people, often the best educated, has been the most serious.

Canadian society has changed so much over the past century that the saying "the government governs best that governs least" has lost most of its validity. Governments at all levels are expected to initiate positive programs for the benefit of citizens, protecting them from economic hazards, compensating them for handicaps, and assuring all a reasonable standard of living. On the other hand, in more recent years a backlash against the role of big government has challenged the concept of government as protector and regulator within a laissez-faire society.

A Period of Reform

The initial post-war change in Canada's circumstances and attitudes posed two alternative paths that government could follow. The first alternative might have led to a reorganization of government, particularly at the local and provincial levels, sufficient to provide the lowest level with the money, manpower, and institutional capacity required to respond to the new demands. The other alternative was to move towards centralization of power, enabling the government with the greatest resources (the federal government) to take on new areas of public sector activity. This latter alternative is the one that became dominant in the post-WWII years, as the federal government used its "powers of the purse" to become steadily more involved in services that the BNA Act of 1867 had assigned to the provincial level. Health care, social assistance, and post-secondary education thereby became targeted by federal policies. The power lay in the ability to provide federal money transfers, while the motivation was directed towards creation of a national social safety net.

In the past decades, there has been some reversal of this centralizing trend. Several provinces, particularly the larger and wealthier ones, have moved to recapture from Ottawa their constitutional authority to deal with matters such as health care, immigration, social services and economic policy. On the other hand, under the pressure of fiscal restraint, Ottawa has been more than eager to decrease its financial contributions to the social programs that had become an increasingly burdensome responsibility.

These developments cause serious concerns in the less wealthy provinces. In the case of the Maritime Provinces, there has been a heavy and continuous dependency on federal programs of regional economic development, as exemplified by the Cape Breton Development Company (DEVCO), the various incarnations of the Federal Department of Regional Economic Expansion, and Atlantic Provinces special funding agencies such as the Atlantic Canada Opportunities Agency (ACOA). Likewise, a serious problem is posed by actual and prospective reductions in transfer payments for support of social assistance programs, post-secondary education and health care services.

Resulting provincial problems in social and economic policy have a spillover effect upon provincial-municipal relations. Municipalities have been caught in a real "fiscal squeeze", a situation in which the demands for services have consistently outstripped the financial capacity to provide them. Even more important, perhaps, has been what might be called a "policy squeeze". As the demands for new and expanded services have increased, municipalities have found themselves increasingly hemmed in by provincial controls which force them to adjust to provincial priorities. The policy squeeze has, in many ways, been the direct result of provincial attempts to reduce the pressure of the fiscal squeeze.

For many years the normal provincial response to the financial problems of municipalities came in the form of grants. These were often conditional grants, subject to substantial supervision and control by the provinces. The attempts to exercise supervision and control have led to many irritations and much bickering, a familiar consequence when one government raises money and another spends it.

New Brunswick's Reform Approach

New Brunswick was the first of the Maritime provinces to embark on an ambitious program of municipal reform. In the early 1960's, a Royal Commission on Finance and Municipal Taxation was set up to examine the financial difficulties of municipalities and their dependent school boards. The Byrne Commission, as it came to be known, reported in 1963 with recommendations for a far reaching redistribution of responsibilities between the province and its local governments. Education, social services, health and the administration of justice were to be transferred to the provincial government. In turn, the report recommended that county municipalities be dissolved and their functions taken over directly by the province.

In 1967, the government brought in its "Program for Equal Opportunities" incorporating most of the measures recommended by the Byrne Commission. Instead of creating bigger or two-tier municipal units as was happening in Ontario, New Brunswick's reforms saw the dismantling of its larger municipalities—the counties—and their partial replacement by dozens of villages as new, smaller municipalities. Outside these villages, the rural sections of the counties ceased to have full-fledged municipal governments and instead received services from local service district administrative offices run by the province. These changes were accompanied by provincial take-over of full responsibility for education, social welfare and health services throughout the province. The remaining towns, cities and villages were left free to levy property taxes to pay for their local services, but administration of property assessments and collection was likewise assumed by the province.

This reform program introduced by Robichaud's Liberal government was shock treatment for a municipal system that had suffered all the ills of New Brunswick's stubborn economic stagnation. Primary resource industries offered few opportunities for young people as technical change meant declining employment. Inadequate opportunities for technical apprenticeship training were barriers to development of new secondary industries. The small and scattered population base, coupled with poor roads and other infrastructure, had added to the bleak prospects facing rural communities in the province.

Municipal reform removed major burdens from local government, but for one third of the population it also removed all local self-government! In the urban areas, the program did little to address issues such as inner core decline, competition among jurisdictions, inadequate land use planning, and the problems of ribbon development beyond town and city boundaries. The drastic changes did not address these issues and thereby contributed to the considerable opposition that helped to defeat the Robichaud government in 1970.

In the years that have followed, attempts have been made to address some of the shortcomings, but the process is far from complete. The lack of representative local governments in rural areas has been partially addressed by encouraging formation of new villages. In the urban areas, attempts have been made to encourage regional units through amalgamation, but only in the case of the new City of Miramichi has this succeeded. The cities of Fredericton, Saint John and Moncton have enlarged their boundaries by annexation of some of their surrounding areas. In the Greater Moncton area, three major urban units (Dieppe, Riverview, and Moncton) have achieved some of the benefits of regionalization of services through inter-municipal co-operation while maintaining their individual structures.

Municipal Reform in Nova Scotia

In Nova Scotia, the Liberal government elected in 1970 set up a Royal Commission under the Chairmanship of Professor John Graham with a broad mandate to examine all aspects of the provincial-municipal relationship and the allocation of service responsibilities between the two levels. After three years of work the Commission reported in a massive series of volumes containing over 6,000 pages. It proposed a comprehensive overhaul of the existing setup, including replacement of the sixty-five existing municipal units by eleven new regional municipalities. The province was to take over all so-called "general services", including education, social services, health, housing and the administration of justice. Various administrative support services such as assessment, tax billing and collection, capital borrowing, staff pension funds, were likewise to be provided by the province.[4]

4 *Report of the Royal Commission on Education, Public Services and Provincial-Municipal Relations.* Halifax: Queen's Printer, 1974.

The Graham Commission's recommendations had initially met with a good deal of public support, receiving praise and favourable comment from a number of municipal officials as well as the public. Over time, however, this was over-ridden by outspoken opposition from influential individuals and organizations, and the government lost heart. The Report was quietly shelved, although over the next two decades, some of its recommendations have surfaced piecemeal and have been enacted into law. Not until the 1990's, however, did fundamental change to basic structures start to emerge.

Under pressure of reduced transfers from Ottawa, the province was forced to review the costs of its programs of support for municipalities. A Task Force on Local Government, set up in 1991, proposed a reallocation of service responsibilities between the two levels, with the province to assume the costs of social services and corrections while rural municipalities would take on those of policing and rural roads. Furthermore, the Report envisaged a process of municipal consolidation in five counties with significant urbanized areas.

Despite earlier predictions that the change of government in 1993 would scuttle the plans for municipal amalgamations in industrial Cape Breton and in Halifax County, events proved that the newly elected Savage administration had become convinced of the wisdom of these reforms. Cape Breton Regional Municipality joined together and replaced the former City of Sydney, the towns of North Sydney, Glace Bay, Dominion, Louisbourg and the rural Municipality of Cape Breton. In Halifax County, the cities of Halifax and Dartmouth, the Town of Bedford, and the Halifax County Municipality were amalgamated into the Halifax Regional Municipality.

While these major amalgamations were proposed and variously defended on the principal grounds that major economies of scale would surely be achieved, events have indicated otherwise. Both of the new Regional Municipalities incurred transitional costs that were far greater than had been forecast. Operational expenses have also been much higher than expected, not least because the combining of municipal staff has resulted in salary levels rising to the highest common denominator!

As part of a municipal reform package, the new Liberal government also adopted the principle of service exchange proposed in the 1992 Task Force Report. A feature of this program was that emergency aid to poorer municipal units would be phased out. In its place, the province would provide a five-year period of transitional payments and, during this time, municipalities would be relieved of responsibility for social welfare services and contributions to the cost of correctional services. In return, rural municipalities would take over the costs of policing and residential streets, these services already being paid for by urban units. A basic principle of the service exchange was to be that the program would have neutral effects on budgets.

These major changes have taken place at the same time that the province has been struggling with its problems of deficit reduction. One of the measures found necessary has been to cap the amount available for equalization payments to financially weak municipal units. In particular, for a number of coastal towns formerly dependent on the ground fishery, the resulting reduction in block grant entitlements has proven to be a grave disaster.

Municipal Reform in Prince Edward Island

In Prince Edward Island, reform debates have centred on land use issues, such as preservation of the agricultural base, non-resident ownership, property taxation and urban-rural tensions. The suburban sprawl outside established urban centres created competition for commercial and industrial assessment, with resulting pressure for boundary revision through amalgamation. As in other provinces, the dramatic increase in the use and ownership of motor vehicles, the abandonment of railway lines, and the massive development of the road network, had all led to profound changes in population distribution and in demands for local services.

The provincial government had responded to the emerging local service needs of its rural areas by enactment, in1950, of the Village Service Act and, in 1967, by the Community Improvement Act. These statutes have enabled small communities to organize local services such as fire protection, garbage collection and disposal, street lighting, and general administration. Prince Edward Island had never had a system of county government, so these Acts were important in filling this void. More than forty of these local units of government have been formed up to the time of writing.

The process of urbanization in the years after the World Wars led to population growth in three major centres, namely the Charlottetown and Summerside areas, and to a lesser extent in the Montague area. But the geographic boundaries of these communities did not change to accommodate this growth. Instead new communities in the urban fringe were incorporated as separate units. When, in 1988, the province chose to achieve some measure of administrative consolidation by placing all forms of local government under a new Municipalities Act, it did not address the consequences of proliferation of new communities around the urban centres.

A problem of this suburbanization arises when the inner core experiences high property values, high tax rates, and commercial displacement of formerly residential areas. Movement to the suburbs tends to cream off those residents best able to pay for the services they need, leaving behind the poor and the elderly who are least able. Lower land values, less traffic congestion and more up-to-date infrastructure also enable suburban municipalities to compete for new and relocating commercial developments.

Such problems were particularly evident in the urbanized areas of the province. In 1990 the Report of the Royal Commission on the Land noted that nine suburbs of the City of Charlottetown had been incorporated as separate communities. The Commission urged that "where the outlying ribbon development begins, so should the municipal borders". The province took the advice to heart, and following the Report of the Commission on Municipal Reform (Charlottetown and Summerside Areas) in late 1993, the government passed legislation to establish three amalgamated units in the Charlottetown area,[5] and at the same time created a single amalgamated city in Summerside.

Municipal Reform: An Ongoing Topic

The reception accorded major municipal reform proposals suggests that Maritimers may be accepting of change, but only at a moderate pace. At the time of writing, the search for further solutions has lost some of its momentum, as all three provinces attempt to digest the public's response to massive municipal amalgamations that had been touted as *the* ideal and final solution.

Summary

The history of the evolution of local government in the Maritime provinces has been described against an overview of the political events and technological and societal changes that have taken place since the middle of the eighteenth century. Only towards the end of the nineteenth century did municipalities based on elected councils become widespread. Once established, the role of these units remained fixed on the provision of a limited range of public services until the post-WWII era brought with it the huge growth of suburban communities. Even then, what had become the traditional framework of local government remained resistant to change.

5 Charlottetown Area Municipalities Act, proclaimed on July 28, 1994, established the expanded City of Charlottetown, and the Towns of Charlottetown South, and Charlottetown West.

Only in the last few decades have some of the provinces sought to restructure their relations with municipal governments so that municipalities might be strong enough to govern without constant and detailed provincial supervision. On the other hand, the arrival of fiscal constraint has changed some of the aims of reform movements. The emphasis has been on reducing fiscal transfers from the provinces to their local governments as well as on downloading of program and service costs from the provincial to the municipal level.

The balance of power in our political system remains with the federal and provincial levels, and municipal governments are finding themselves, especially in urban areas, increasingly the centre of political debate and controversy. In the interests of greater efficiency, the provinces have sought to reduce the number of municipal units through amalgamation of autonomous suburbs with their urban centres. The result of such policies is seen in the creation of the City of Miramichi in New Brunswick, the Cape Breton Regional Municipality and the Halifax Regional Municipality in Nova Scotia, and the new City of Summerside and the three newly consolidated units in the Charlottetown area of Prince Edward Island.

This brief historical overview has been offered to assist the reader in gaining a better understanding of how some of the existing structures and functions have evolved, as well as the pressures towards change.

Chapter II

Local Government in the Scheme of Things[1]

Introduction

Local government is often viewed in terms of the public services necessary for day-to-day life, whether in cities, towns, villages, or even rural communities. Street and sidewalk maintenance, police and fire protection, water supply, parks and playgrounds, garbage and sewage disposal —services that we most often take for granted, but which are essential if we are to function in a modern society.

In addition to providing such housekeeping services, the local level of government has a political role that should not be underestimated. It occupies a key position within the complex structure of federal, provincial and local public institutions that serve to regulate, protect, promote and mediate the diverse interests of citizens in our society. Relations among the three governmental levels are complex, perplexing and often subject to strains and stresses. As the most junior level, local government has little independent jurisdiction, but as the level "closest to the people", some of its primary power lies in its potential for mobilizing public opinion.

Constitutional and Statutory Principles

Our formal constitution, the Constitution Act 1982, guarantees no independent powers to Canadian municipalities. Indeed, the BNA Act of 1867 (now retitled the Constitution Act 1867) granted the provinces exclusive jurisdiction over all municipal institutions. Therefore, in a legal sense, local governments are totally subordinate to their provincial overlords and have often been called "creatures" of the provinces.

1 Parts of this chapter are based on text prepared by Professor David M. Cameron for *A Guide to Local Government in Nova Scotia, First Edition*, Halifax, 1977.

The legal authority of local government therefore rests exclusively on powers assigned by provincial legislation. A key principle emerges from this status: municipal governments may not legally do anything which the parent provincial government has not specifically empowered them to do. Furthermore, any such power can be withdrawn by the province at any time.

This may seem to suggest that municipalities play only a limited and secondary role in the process of government. Before we jump to that conclusion, however, it is important to consider other possible sources of governmental power.

Social and Political Power

Neither the constitution nor provincial statutes tell the whole story of the status of municipal government. Any government in a democratic system derives its fundamental power from its electorate. Electorates of the three government levels in Canada overlap, so that voters have the ultimate power to shape legislative decisions. It follows that the more effective a particular municipal government is in responding to the needs and desires of its citizens, the more secure its political position is likely to be.

As municipal councillors generally have a close and continuous relationship with the communities they represent, local government has the image of being the "grassroots" level of democracy. The actions of councils are readily visible to all citizens, and therefore people tend to accept the local level as the most available of their governments. Because of this, it has long been assumed that public opinion places some constraint on the ability of any province to deal arbitrarily with its municipal organizations. Recent moves by several provincial governments to impose sweeping amalgamations on their more highly urbanized areas seem to run counter to this assumption, but the final judgement by the electorate on such "reforms" must await the outcome of subsequent provincial elections.

In any case, it is clear that local governments cannot be considered in isolation from the provincial and the federal levels. Canadian society has become so complex and interdependent that informal relations between governments are often more important than indicated by the constitutional or legislative framework.

Definitions

"Municipalities" are the most common form of local governmental units.[3] They are "corporate" bodies, created under the terms of provincial legislation providing for a process of incorporation, hence the term "incorporated" municipality. Most Canadians live within a "municipal unit". Cities and towns are the most familiar examples. More sparsely settled areas in New Brunswick and Prince Edward Island do not have municipal government, but Nova Scotia's territory is completely organized under some form of municipal unit.

The term "local government" may be used to cover other types of units besides "municipalities", including various "local special-purpose bodies", such as police commissions, hospital boards, regulatory commissions, library boards, planning commissions, and boards to operate anything from bridges to recreational centres. Some such bodies may be created directly by provincial legislation, while others may be formed under powers delegated to municipalities.

How Local Government Differs from Senior Levels

The federal and provincial governments in Canada resemble each other in many ways. Municipalities, however, are very different in structure. The most obvious variance is that there are only two, rather than three, distinctive branches or functions at the local level. The senior levels each have a legislative, an executive and a judicial branch. The judicial branch has almost completely disappeared at the local level, even though, as noted in Chapter I, in early times the local government was the "Court" of Sessions. Mayors of cities and towns may still be referred to as "chief magistrates", but that label is merely a reminder of a bygone institution.

The terms "legislative" and "executive" branches are not often used with reference to local government. Instead of branches, we speak of functions, such as the "policy-making" function, and the "administrative" function. Despite this switch in labels, the local policy-making structure, or Council, has the same purpose as a legislative branch in the other levels, and the local administrative structure corresponds to the executive branch in the federal or provincial governments.

Policy-making in municipalities is intended to be the main function of the elected officials. They make local policy according to the powers and responsibilities delegated explicitly to them by provincial legislation. In

3 Note that in Nova Scotia, the term "municipality" has become descriptive of county or rural district units.

law, they can make no decisions beyond those defined in the provincial legislation under which they operate. And whatever powers and responsibilities the province does delegate can be changed, removed, or added to at any time unilaterally by the provincial government.

The local policy-making function is associated primarily with *elected* officials, while the *appointed* officials are mainly involved with administrative matters. The elected officials include the mayor (or warden or chairpersons) and the councillors. Canadian mayors are normally not "strong" mayors in terms of the legal powers and responsibilities delegated to them by provincial legislation, but depending on their personal characteristics, they may still have a strong influence on the policy process. Basically, they chair all meetings of council, are usually ex officio members of all committees of council, perform ceremonial functions, and represent the municipality in negotiations with the provincial government.

Partly because the delegated policy-making powers and responsibilities of local government are indeed changed from time to time, it is not possible to be precise in listing them. Moreover, municipalities even within one province do not all have the same list of powers. Generally, "regional municipalities" and "city" municipalities are delegated more powers than "town" municipalities, which in turn have somewhat more powers than those of "county" or other small or rural municipalities. Furthermore, *exclusive* powers or responsibilities are rarely delegated to the municipalities. For example, many council decisions that municipalities are permitted to make do not become law until approved by the provincial Minister responsible for municipal affairs. Also, some council decisions, (especially those dealing with land use planning), can be appealed to a provincial tribunal having the legal power to review and eventually overturn such decisions.

Despite variations within a province and between provinces, the significant powers delegated to municipalities usually include matters involving "services to property": roads and sidewalks, street lighting, water supply, sewage collection and treatment, garbage collection and disposal, land use (including zoning and the issuance of development and building permits), fire and other property protection. The provinces generally delegate to municipal councils a relatively modest policy-making role, reserving to themselves the more important policy decisions involving general services. Local government's role in some matters is often that of being an administrative agency acting on behalf of the provincial government.

External Relations

We have already considered a number of matters that have important bearing on intergovernmental relations from the local perspective. First is the fact that according to the Canadian Constitution, local government is a provincial responsibility. Consequently, relations between local government and the federal government of Canada are usually indirect—through the provincial government—rather than direct. But even with this reservation, the federal influence in our communities and in municipal offices is of substantial importance and may profoundly affect the functioning of this level of government.

Federal Relations

At the policy level, federal program initiatives often have important consequences for local government. A few examples will illustrate this relationship. If a new federal budget concentrates on deficit reduction, municipalities may find themselves facing problems resulting from increased unemployment. Policy changes in the name of fighting inflation may increase the interest rate on municipal borrowing. On the other hand, communities may benefit from regional development policies which may result in growth of their industrial sector, thereby leading to an increase in the municipal tax base.

All too often, however, outside industries fail when subsidies and resources run out and municipalities may find themselves saddled with new facilities, such as overbuilt water and sewage treatment plants. Communities such as Glace Bay, Port Hawkesbury, Chatham, and many other Maritime locales are living monuments to federal efforts that have ended in municipal misfortune.

Historically, the federal government has played an essential role in equalizing the ability of provincial governments to provide a basic standard of services. Ever since Confederation, the Maritime provinces have relied heavily on federal transfer payments to enable them to keep up with wealthier provinces. In recent years, however, these transfers have not fully kept up with increases in the costs of providing services. In turn, the provinces have drawn back on their municipal equalization grant monies. The municipalities then become the level who have to "bite the bullet" in finding places to be cut in consequence of federal restraint.

Not all federal impacts are indirect. Municipalities receive some conditional grant financing from the federal government for "infrastructure" such as public housing, sewage treatment, road building and upgrading, and even for golf courses! Likewise, "payments in lieu" of property tax on federally-owned property may add substantially to municipal revenues in the communities where such property is located. When the federal activities involves major military installations, port facilities, airfields, research institutes, national parks, and many other activity centres, the municipality is an obvious provider of services (and collector of property taxes) from the employees of these federal enterprises.

For obvious reasons, then, municipalities must maintain some level of liaison with the federal government. They do so both collectively (through the Federation of Canadian Municipalities in particular) and individually. Apart from federal agencies resident in the community, the Canada Mortgage and Housing Corporation remains a key source of technical information on a wide range of municipal concerns in the building and development field, and is also an important player in housing programs.

Municipal-Provincial Relations

Not least because of their constitutional dependence, municipalities must, of necessity, maintain active links with their provincial government. As noted earlier, local governmental units are generally not delegated exclusive powers in many of the services that they provide. They must often act as administrative agencies of the provincial government, especially for services related to people rather than those more directly related to property.

As a consequence, there is constant communication between municipal offices and provincial departments. Examples include departments responsible for provincial police and their relations with municipal police departments, the provincial Fire Marshall regarding local fire services, provincial education authorities regarding public school finances, the provincial highways departments regarding municipal streets and roads, the provincial welfare departments regarding social services, provincial recreation and cultural agencies with their municipal counterparts, and provincial departments with environmental responsibilities regarding local water supply, sewage treatment matters and environmental pollution.

Much of such interaction focuses on financial arrangements with the province on "cost shared" programs, where the province pays a specified portion of the costs and local government pays the rest. In order to make sure that its money is spent the way it wants, the provincial government sets standards and sees that they are heeded by the local authorities. Apart from such direct and often informal communication, there are also situations where interaction is more formal or collective, that is, between an association of municipalities on the one hand and a provincial minister or his or her officials on the other.

Relations with Departments Responsible for Municipal Affairs

Initially, municipal affairs departments were set up primarily as financial watchdogs over the day-to-day operations of local government. This watchdog role continues, but over the years the Departments have developed into broader resource centres for local governments, providing information, research and advice, and often acting as advocates and interveners on behalf of the individual municipalities.

In matters of assessment for property tax purposes, there is a whole field of provincial-municipal relationships that will be dealt with elsewhere in this book. For the moment, it is enough to recall that in the Maritime provinces, the assessment function is a technical service provided by each province. But municipal councils are very sensitive to the quality of assessments, not only because citizens are often hazy about who is responsible for their property valuations, but also because the municipal assessment roll is a key element in the calculation of provincial grants for both general and specific purposes.

Issue-Related Relationships

Beyond regular "day-to-day" interaction between the two levels, there are also "issue-by-issue" matters that may have to be dealt with more formally, including cases that come before a provincial tribunal, such as the Utility and Review Board in Nova Scotia or to the courts of any of the provinces. Examples include appeals taken by property owners against municipal planning decisions, or applications for annexation of territory to a town or city. A somewhat different example of issue-by-issue interaction would be a provincial enquiry into major local issues such as problems in a town's police force; an environmental enquiry into methods of sewage disposal; or a task force approach to determine the future location of a landfill facility.

As the above examples suggest, issue-by-issue and day-to-day interaction obviously makes for a very complex provincial-local relationship, with subjects ranging from purely administrative matters to emotionally-charged political topics. The subject of it all is not always money, although economic interests are often involved.

Relations Among Local Governmental Units

Within most localities there is, of course, more than a single local governmental unit. Besides the municipal council, there is likely to be all or part of a school district, one or more local special-purpose bodies such as a public utilities commission, a library board, a commission to operate an arena or convention facility, a separately incorporated volunteer fire company, and so on. Some of these special-purpose bodies may have inherited considerable autonomy and be largely beyond control of municipal council. If local government is required to carry or contribute to their costs, however, co-ordination of their budgetary process is obviously desirable. In the same way, if a municipality's planning department is expecting new residential subdivisions to develop in a particular place, other agencies such as the school board, recreation organizations, the library board and the public utilities authority all need to have such information.

Another setting for relations among local governmental units involves neighbouring communities. Adjacent municipalities must often seek to co-ordinate their actions and plans. Obviously, it is undesirable for one municipal council to decide to construct a major new sewer outfall immediately upstream from an adjacent municipality's water supply intake. Similarly, the construction of a new industrial park or residential suburb in one municipality may have serious impact on traffic in other municipalities. Neighbouring municipalities need to co-ordinate their emergency measures operations to plan, for example, for the most logical placement of their fire stations.

Association Relationships

Local governments in all the provinces have formed organizations that provide a number of invaluable services. First, they represent their member municipalities in discussions and negotiations with senior governments. Speaking with the united voice of their member units, these associations have, over the years, had considerable influence on policies of both federal and provincial governments. Second, the associations collect data and distribute information not otherwise available to their members. Third, the annual meetings of the organizations provide an opportunity for local officials to meet together to exchange views and experiences. These gatherings also provide opportunities for informing the media on municipally-related topics of concern to all Canadians.

Federation of Canadian Municipalities (FCM)

The Federation of Canadian Municipalities is the national voice of local government. Most municipal units in Canada are members of this organization. It has played a significant role as the champion of local government in relations with the federal level. Among its most recent achievements are the successful conclusion of a modification of the Goods and Services Tax, which resulted in substantial rebates of municipal expenditures on this tax; its work in updating legislation with respect to payments in lieu of taxation of federal properties; the success in gaining acceptance for the program of infrastructure grants for the upgrading of municipal facilities, and generally in keeping both the federal government and the public aware of the needs of local government.

Provincial Organizations of Municipalities

Throughout the Maritimes, municipal units are represented by organizations which, over the years, have been effective voices in relations with provincial authorities. In Nova Scotia, the Union of Nova Scotia Municipalities has been in existence for almost a century, during which time it has been an important factor in keeping local government issues before provincial authorities. In recent times, it has been effective in clarifying provincial policies with respect to the service exchange program. In New Brunswick, The Cities Association, and the Union of Municipalities of New Brunswick, play very simipar roles.

The Municipal Research and Information Centre

This organization, with headquarters in Fredericton, NB, was first formed under the auspices of the now defunct New Brunswick Provincial-Municipal Council. The Centre has subsequently been separately incorporated and is funded by fees from subscribing members in all three Maritime provinces. The data collected by the Centre has gone a long way towards providing a level informational playing field for municipalities in collective bargaining negotiations with national and international unions representing their employees. Another active association in New Brunswick is the francophone "l'Association des municipalitiés du Nouveau-Brunswick". The Federation of Prince Edward Island Municipalities is the voice of local governments in that province.

Professional Organizations

A significant factor in the development of better educated and qualified administrative leaders in the Maritime Provinces has been the formation of provincial organizations primarily devoted to professional upgrading. The first of these was the Association of Municipal Administrators, Nova Scotia, formed in 1969 by the first class of municipal clerks and deputies to graduate from a four-year correspondence course offered by the Institute of Public Affairs at Dalhousie University. New Brunswick and Prince Edward Island graduates of this course subsequently formed similar organizations. All three of these professional associations have developed their own programs and co-operate with educational institutions in sponsoring and conducting a variety of annual conferences, seminars, and short courses. These activities have fostered a sense of self-esteem and have produced a high standard of professional competence among municipal administrators in the Maritimes.

In 1974, the Council of Maritime Premiers established the Maritime Municipal Training and Development Board (MMTDB) as a means of promoting and funding professional development programs. The Board has been a highly effective source of information and encouragement for the kind of "boot-strap" administrative upgrading that has taken place since the early 1970's. It has worked closely with academic institutions in development of both non-credit and degree programs in municipal public adminstration.

The Local Politician: Policy Maker, Decision Maker, Mediator

The changes in intergovernmental relationships are among many other changes that have resulted in a changed and perplexing role for the local politician. The traditional function of the politician as administrator, providing the highest possible level of services at the lowest possible cost, has now largely disappeared. Local governments must now deal with conflicting demands for express-ways and public transit, for the development and preservation of neighbourhoods, for social security and employment creation, for industrial growth and environmental protection, for economic development and a higher quality of life. These are seldom either/or choices, and elected officials must seek to grapple with the fundamental values that are at stake.

Society has thus placed an enormous responsibility upon its municipal politicians. They must be mediators seeking to reconcile conflicting demands from citizens, often without the resources to fully satisfy most demands. They must also be decision makers, because ultimately conflicts must be resolved (or at least managed) and actions undertaken.

It is here that the challenge to the local politician becomes clear. The pressure and demands on local government are real, profound, and unlikely to go away. If council members will not respond to such demands and pressures, then others will. These others will include private interests, appointed officials, or politicians at other levels of government, and citizens will lose the opportunity for shaping their community through their own elected local representatives. In short, if local politicians do not rise to the challenge of their changed and changing role in a complex society, local citizens will be the losers.

Summary

The subservience of municipal governments to provincial authority is entrenched in the Canadian Constitution and recurs as a dominant factor in the evolution of local governments in the Maritime provinces. Yet the urge for local self-government remains as something to be reckoned with, even as the provinces seek to impose their own priorities.

The needs of Maritime communities have undergone enormous changes in the years since municipal institutions first came into being. These changes have brought new demands and responsibilities to local governments. The most significant consequence has been a transition from being purely providers of a few basic services to new roles as caretakers of the environment, promoters of community development, and mediators among the typical variety of competing interests in the community. In carrying out these old and new responsibilities, the elected councillors of local government continue their long established task of managing growing responsibilities with often shrinking resources.

This chapter has provided an outline of how local governments have been structured to deal with their responsibilities; how their activities are affected by relations with the federal level and with the various programs and policies of their parent provinces. We have touched on relations between neighbouring municipalities and within the organizations that speak on behalf of local governments generally. Finally, we have spoken of the key role played by elected municipal officials in this complex web of local government relationships.

Chapter III

Local Government and the Law

The "rule of law" is the essence of the national state whose fundamental function is to provide justice and protection for all its citizens. In a democratic society, protection extends not only to external and internal threats, but assures the individual the right to enjoy personal liberties free from discrimination or arbitrary limitation by governments.

Introduction

The Canadian Constitution defines relationships between the federal, provincial and municipal levels of government. The Constitution also covers safeguards intended to shield individuals from despotic or arbitrary actions of any level of government.

The legal framework of local government in each province is established by provincial legislation, including the powers delegated to municipal councils to set policy and administer at the local level.

The elected members of municipal councils must maintain an awareness of the legal relationships that exist among all three levels of government in Canada. It is not enough to be familiar only with those statutes that are specific to the municipal level. What local government can do is governed by a broad variety of both federal and provincial laws as well as by the interpretations given to laws by judicial decisions.

The Constitution of Canada, Federal Law, and Local Government

Canada's first Constitution, the British North America Act, or BNA Act, was an Act of the British Parliament that came into force in 1867. Up until 1982, the Constitution could only be modified or changed by amendment passed by the British House of Commons and the House of Lords in London. After more than a century of discussion and negotiation between the federal and provincial governments in Canada, it was finally agreed that the British Parliament should be asked to pass an amendment that would transfer power over the constitution to Canada. As a result, the Constitution Act 1982 did just that. This was an important change from the original BNA Act of 1867. By "patriating" the legislation, it means that we no longer need to apply to the parliament of the United Kingdom to obtain changes in our constitution. One serious problem arose in the process, however, in that the Province of Quebec had not registered its approval of the terms of the patriation and the provisions for future amendments.

All parts of the original BNA Act defining the division of powers between the federal and provincial governments were continued in the Constitution Act 1982. One of the sections specifies that provinces are to have full jurisdiction over municipal institutions. The legal authority of local government is thus based on powers assigned by legislation enacted by provincial legislatures.

The Canadian Charter of Rights and Freedoms

The 1982 Act goes well beyond merely continuing the original division of powers in the federal-provincial relationship. In adding a "Canadian Charter of Rights and Freedoms", the Constitution now expresses a number of basic rights guaranteed to individuals in relations with their governments. These provisions apply to the Government of Canada and the Territories, as well as to the governments of each province "in respect of all matters within the authority of the legislature of each province". Under the latter clause, local government is obviously included. It should be noted, however, that the Charter deals with obligations of governments towards people, but does not cover relationships between individuals or their rights with respect to businesses.

While all sections of the Charter apply to governments in general, certain sections are particularly pertinent to the municipal level. Awareness of the whole Charter will help to guide council members in making decisions related to a variety of matters. Examples of questions that may arise include: use of municipal premises for public meetings; affirmative action in hiring policies; zoning by-laws; housing assistance; access provisions for the disabled in public buildings; policing and by-law enforcement in general. Sections that may be applicable in these respects are worth particular attention and are reviewed in the next few paragraphs.

The "fundamental freedoms" protected under the Charter appear in Section 2:

> *2. Everyone has the following fundamental freedoms:*
> *(a) freedom of conscience and religion;*
> *(b) freedom of thought, belief, opinion and expression, including freedom of the press and other media of communication;*
> *(c) freedom of peaceful assembly; and*
> *(d) freedom of association.*

It is interesting to note that the term "everyone" has been interpreted by the Supreme Court of Canada to include not only persons, but has also been applied to corporate bodies. Thus, in the Court's decisions in the cases of the Irving Toy company and in the challenge to the Tobacco Products Restraint Act, it was ruled that commercial advertising is protected by 2 (b). This illustrates how the intentions of legislators may be modified by subsequent judicial interpretation.

Section 15 of the Charter guarantees "equality rights":

> *Every individual is equal before and under the law and has the right to the equal protection and equal benefit of the law without discrimination and, in particular, without discrimination based on race, national or ethnic origin, colour, religion, sex, age or mental and physical disability.*

Sections 7 to 14 speak to legal rights that provide safeguards against unreasonable search and seizure, arbitrary detention or imprisonment, prohibition against cruel and unusual treatment and punishment, and for due process of law *"in accordance with the principles of fundamental justice"*. These safeguards have particular significance for all municipal councils who have responsibility for police departments or by-law enforcement officers. Taken together with non-discrimination guarantees in Section 15, for example, these stated rights lend emphasis to the findings of the judicial enquiry into the circumstances of the Marshall trial and his conviction for a murder that he did not commit.[1]

Other entrenched rights in the Charter include guarantees with respect to official languages in federal departments, agencies and proceedings; other minority language and educational rights, and inter-provincial mobility.

1 *Royal Commission on the Donald Marshall, Jr. Prosecution: Commissioner's Report: findings and recommendations*. Halifax: Queen's Printer, 1989.

The Charter allows a certain latitude to governments by specifying that the Charter's guarantees of rights and freedoms are *"subject only to such reasonable limits prescribed by law as can be demonstrably justified in a free and democratic society"*. The interpretation of "reasonable limits" is an aspect of the Charter that has created a greatly expanded constitutional role for the Supreme Court of Canada. This is not an entirely new role for the Court, however. Since 1867, judicial decisions on a range of matters have shaped the meaning of the original British North America Act, so that as presently interpreted it would hardly be recognizable by the original "Fathers of Confederation". Judicial interpretation (or case law) has thus been a potent source of the law of the constitution, a process that seems likely to continue indefinitely.

Other Federal Laws and Municipal Government

The Canadian Constitution is obviously part of the legal environment of all governmental bodies, but many other federal statutes govern matters of concern to the municipal level. These range over subjects such as the criminal code, human rights, consumer protection, transportation and communication, environmental regulation, economic development, housing and a variety of other matters.

Apart from emphasizing the need for municipal councils to maintain an awareness that they are part of the entire fabric of Canadian governmental law, it is well beyond the scope of this book to attempt a review of the huge body of federal legislation that may have relevance for municipal decision making.

Local Government and Provincial Law

As noted earlier, the Constitution Act is the source of the exclusive provincial power to legislate with respect to local government. Municipal units therefore are organized and administered under provincial legislation and have only such powers as specifically conferred by statute. A town council could not, for example, decide to go into the grocery business, since there is no statute giving it such authority. Should the town actually enter into such business and lose money, councillors who, in the name of the town, authorized the business could well be held personally liable to the town for such loss. But note, on the other hand, that if the business were to make money, the profit would belong to the town!

It follows that in order to exercise any function, a municipal corporation must find its authority in the relevant statute or regulation made under the statute. As a rule, statutes spell out the specific responsibilities assigned to municipal corporations. Under a general clause covering matters "incidental to carrying out duties and responsibilities", it might appear that councils could interpret their jurisdiction very broadly, but authority derived from such general power has only limited application in any province.

Types of Municipal Organizations

There are a variety of municipal units incorporated by statutes in the Maritime provinces. Some of the existing bodies include:

Cities and Regional Municipalities

In Nova Scotia, the Cape Breton Regional Municipality and the Halifax Regional Municipality, each created by individual Acts of the provincial legislature enacted in 1995, introduced a new form of urban organization centred on existing city units. This provincial program of municipal reform through mandatory amalgamation had the avowed purpose of reducing administrative costs of too many municipal units. The reforms were imposed by the provincial level, often in the face of strong resistance by the affected communities and their existing municipal councils. The amalgamation of the Town of Liverpool and the Municipality of Queens County, on the other hand, was achieved through voluntary action within the two local governments.

In New Brunswick, the City of Saint John, the earliest municipal unit in British North America, was incorporated by Royal Charter in 1785. Provincial charters subsequently established the cities of Fredericton (1848), Moncton (1890), Edmundston (1952), Bathurst (1956), and Campbellton (1958). The boundaries of these cities have often been expanded by amalgamation and annexation of nearby towns and villages. In 1995, the Province created the new City of Miramichi, through the amalgamation of the towns of Chatham, Newcastle and a number of villages and Local Service Districts.

In Prince Edward Island, the City of Charlottetown was created in 1855 by the Charlottetown Act. Its borders remained largely unchanged until 1994 when a major program of amalgamation added a number of neighbouring municipalities to the City, at the same time creating two new towns from neighbouring suburbs.[2] In the same year, the proclamation of the City of Summerside Act effected the amalgamation of

2 Charlottetown Area Municipalities Act, PEI 1994, c.6.

adjacent communities with the former Town of Summerside to give the Province of Prince Edward Island its second city.[3]

Towns

In the three Maritime provinces, towns have been incorporated either by individual legislative Acts or by general legislation such as the Nova Scotia Towns Act or the New Brunswick Towns Act.[4] In Prince Edward Island, Summerside had been the first town incorporated with its own Act, but more recently other towns or communities have been incorporated under the general Municipalities Act.

Rural Local Government

In Nova Scotia, municipalities, sometimes referred to as "rural municipalities", are covered by the Municipal Act.[5] All areas of the province, with the exception of the regional municipalities and the incorporated towns, are included in these county or district municipal units. When denser population centres develop within such rural areas, residents often seek ways to gain more direct influence on matters such as fire protection, recreation, sidewalks, or street lighting. Such communities may apply for the creation of a village service commission under the relevant legislation.

In New Brunswick, rural county government was abolished by the reforms of the "Equal Opportunities" program. Services are provided to rural areas by a system of Local Service Districts administered by the Department responsible for municipal affairs. Over 80 villages have been incorporated where population densities require a higher level of services under the control of elected councils.

In Prince Edward Island, towns and communities are governed by the Municipalities Act.[6] Former villages have been brought under the "community" designation. They differ in structure from towns mainly in the requirement that their annual budgets must be ratified by a meeting of all their residents.

3 City of Summerside Act, PEI 1994, c.59.
4 Towns Act, *R.S.N.S., 1989*, c.472, with subsequent amendments.
5 Municipal Act, *R.S.N.S., 1989*, c.265, with subsequent amendments.
6 Municipalities Act, *R.S.P.E.I., 1988*, Cap. M-13, with subsequent amendments.

Community Councils

The Nova Scotia version of the Community Council concept had its origins in the former Halifax County Municipality. It arose as a result of demands by residents of urbanizing areas of the County for greater direct say in community development and local service delivery. This need was initially expressed as a movement to have the community of Sackville incorporated as a Town or City, separate from the County Municipality. Our 1987 study undertaken for the County,[7] concluded that Sackville's withdrawal would cause major disruption for the County, while property tax rates within the new unit would rise sharply. As an alternative to separation, we advanced the idea of a "county town", still part of the existing municipality, with its council made up of the County council members from districts within the Sackville area. This council would deal with services of primary concern to the local residents of the included districts, but its members would continue as full members of the overall County Council. Administrative services would be provided by the County, so that no separate administration would be required.

The Community Council proposal was endorsed in a plebiscite of Sackville residents in early 1988. Accordingly, five councillors from districts in the Sackville area were, by administrative resolution of the County Council, authorized to meet as a community council. They were empowered to recommend on matters of local concern, particularly in the field of planning and recreation, and on area rates for services not included in the County's general rate. A satellite office was set up in Sackville to provide direct communication with all County departments. Following a period of successful operation in Sackville, a similar community council structure was installed in the Cole Harbour/Westphal area of the County.

The public acceptance of these first two community councils resulted in having the approach included in a new charter for the Halifax County Municipality. Following the 1993 provincial election, the concept was incorporated into legislation establishing regional municipalities in industrial Cape Breton and in the Halifax metropolitan area. Five Community Councils are now operational within the Halifax Regional Municipality, but at publication date, no Community Council has been set up elsewhere in the province.

In Prince Edward Island, the term "community council" has been applied to the rural communities first established under the Community

7 Kell Antoft and Jack Novack. *Urban Areas Study. Study for the Municipality of the County of Halifax.* Halifax: Henson College, June 1987.

Improvement Act of 1967 and continued in the 1988 Municipalities Act. These are a junior level of local governance in rural areas of the province, having jurisdiction over a limited set of services, chiefly fire protection, garbage collection and disposal, street lighting, and general administration.

Special Purpose Boards and Commissions

In addition to the foregoing examples of municipal decision-making bodies, there are special purpose service commissions which function in a limited way like municipalities. These commissions are usually set up by special statute. Examples include commissions created to administer a water utility of the municipality, or those designated to manage parks, rinks, cemeteries, as well as those set up for a particular function such as recreation or tourist promotion. There are also service commissions created to look after services owned and managed by two or more municipal units, such as joint planning commissions, industrial development commissions, and regional hospital boards serving two or more municipal units.

Regulations Under Statutes

As with all legislation, any statute affecting municipalities first appears as a Bill introduced into the provincial legislature by the government of the day. After a process of debate and possible amendment, the Bill becomes an Act when it is passed by majority vote and receives formal assent by the Lieutenant Governor. If the Act contains a requirement for proclamation at a later date, it does not become law until it is proclaimed. For a variety of reasons, a government may withhold this final step for a period of months or even years, although most Acts are in effect when assent is given.

Most statutes, or legislative Acts, contain one or more sections empowering the government to issue regulations to describe in greater detail how the Act is to be administered or its provisions enforced. Such regulations may be minor instructions on matters such as forms or deadlines for filing of reports, or they may contain many pages of technical specifications, such as subdivision regulations under provincial planning statutes. Regulations may also provide authority for a Minister or other agent of the Crown to take specific actions required to give effect to any provision of the Act.

When a statute delegates power to a municipality on any particular subject, the authority is often spelled out as the power to regulate. In effect local governments exercise a large variety of regulatory powers, including matters such as animal control, unsightly premises, hours of business, parking restrictions, garbage collection and recycling, and many others. Depending upon the matter to be regulated, municipal decisions may be in the form of a by-law, a resolution, or by instruction to municipal staff to see that the required action is taken.

Local Government Legislation

An important feature of municipal law is the power of the municipal council to make by-laws.[8] These are laws which carry the same legal authority within a city, town, or other municipal unit as if they had been made by the Legislature. In each of the three provinces, enabling municipal legislation generally sets forth lists of subjects on which councils or service commissions may make by-laws. These lists often are both long and specific. The powers range amongst many and diverse matters over which local authority may be exercised. A few examples will demonstrate their scope: employee pension plans; disposal of records; regulation of chimney sweeps; setting curfew hours for children; regulating early closing times for shops; enforcing building codes; and numerous equally interesting powers.

Councils' by-law authority is not confined to general municipal legislation. There are also examples to be found in provincial statutes dealing with a variety of other topics. For example, in Nova Scotia the power to make by-laws with respect to the licencing and regulating of taxi-cabs is found in the Motor Vehicle Act, and by-law powers relating to municipal policing functions may be found in provincial police legislation. The power to enact by-laws varies among municipalities in each of the Maritime provinces and the size and type of municipal body may determine the subjects on which councils may legislate. It should be kept in mind that some types of by-laws may be subject to the approval of the Minister responsible for municipal matters before coming into effect.

Legal Basis for Expenditures

For each type of municipal unit, the appropriate statute in all provinces generally lists purposes for which councils may budget and authorize expenditures. As with by-law making authority, other statutes relating to

8 The term by-law has sometimes been erroneously described as a lower or junior order of legislation, in the same way that *by-product, by-way* or *by-stander* suggests something of lesser importance. In fact the term originates from the Scandinavian word *by,* which means "settlement", "town" or "city". It is reflected in many place names in the U.K. where the Danes settled in medieval times, e.g., Whitby, Danby, Tornby, etc. Thus by-law is town (or local) law.

particular topics may spell out additional spending powers for local governments. For example, one part of the Nova Scotia Agriculture and Marketing Act contains a section enabling municipal units to make grants to agricultural exhibitions.

Legal Basis for Revenues

Legislation such as provincial Municipal Acts, Towns Acts, and City Charters delegate to respective councils the power to "vote, rate, collect, receive, and appropriate" funds necessary to carry out the legal activities of the municipal unit.

There are three principal sources of revenue available to local governments in the Maritime provinces: the property tax; user fees; and grants from provincial and federal governments. We will consider each of these in turn.

Property Tax

The property tax is a levy based on the value of property. Determining this value and preparing the "assessment roll" involves the *assessment process.* Authority for this process is set forth in provincial assessment legislation, a subject to be discussed in detail in Chapter VII.

The tax levied on value is often expressed in various terms. In some jurisdictions elsewhere in North America, the tax rate is stated as a percentage of assessed value. In others it appears as a "mill rate", or as a rate in dollars and cents per $1000 of value. In the Maritime provinces, the words *tax rate* means the amount levied per $100 of the value of each property listed on the assessment roll. Whatever term is used, the principle is the same. For local government purposes, the rate is set each year to collect the amount of tax needed to meet the operating budget of a particular municipal unit.

In addition to municipal needs, provincial governments also use the property tax to help finance services such as education or social services. In New Brunswick and Prince Edward Island, assessment of property as well as the collection of both municipal and provincial tax is a provincial function. The municipal share of the total receipts is forwarded to the individual municipal units in accordance with the tax rates each has adopted in their annual budget.

In Nova Scotia, assessment is also a provincial function, but collection of property taxes is assigned to the municipal units. The province sets its own education property tax rate that municipalities must collect and also specifies how much each municipality must produce in support of provincially-administered services such as justice and social assistance programs. Each municipality must include these levies more or less buried within their own tax bills. As an illustration of the reality of the "creatures of the province" concept, the resulting mandatory provincial property tax levy allows no room for discretion by municipal councillors.

User Fees

User fees are based on direct charges for services provided by the municipal unit. Examples include billing for water supplied by the municipality or its utility commission, fares charged by a public transit system, local improvement charges for sidewalks or curbs, tipping fees for refuse brought to the local landfill site, and charges for admission to, or participation in, recreational events or programs. Authority to enact by-laws covering such user fees is usually set forth in the appropriate provincial legislation. Charges for some municipal services, such as water and electricity, are subject to the approval by provincial regulatory boards. Area rates, based on property assessment, are a particular form of user charges that may be levied in areas of the municipality benefiting from the specified service delivery.

Grants

Provincial grants to municipalities are governed by legislative Acts and by allocations made in the annual budgets. They generally are of three types.

The first type includes all *conditional* grants. These are transfers of monies earmarked for specific purposes. A main condition is that the monies must be expended for services that meet provincially-determined criteria. Often a condition is that part of the costs must be raised within the municipal unit. These conditional grants are an effective method of encouraging local governments to act in accordance with provincial policies and priorities. Purposes have included economic development activities, implementation of uniform environmental protection standards, the maintenance of provincial goals for recreational programs and facilities, and achieving province wide policing, fire protection, planning and other standards.

A second type is the *unconditional* block grant. Such grants are primarily designed to even out the ability of municipal units within a province to provide local services at reasonably comparable levels. These grants recognize disparities in the ability of councils to provide adequate service levels from their own revenue sources. The "ability to pay" is gauged from property assessment values within the local council's jurisdiction. In apportioning provincial grant funds among the local units, the cost of a standard set of municipal services within the various classes of municipalities is calculated. Units whose ability to pay falls short are alloted grant amounts sufficient to bring them up to the provincially-determined standard. The local council remains free to determine how these unconditional allocations are to be spent.

Grants-in-lieu of taxation, the third type, are intended to compensate municipalities for government-owned property that is legally exempt from regular property taxation. Provincial grants of this type vary from province to province and the basis for calculation often varies from year to year. Federal payments "in lieu of taxes" are paid with respect to property owned by Crown corporations or by the senior government directly. Futher details of grant systems will be discussed in Chapter VII.

Other Revenues

Licence and permit fees, income from interest on invested funds, and other miscellaneous revenue sources are generally covered by specific authority contained in legislation for each type of municipal unit within the respective provinces.

Remuneration of Elected Officials

The remuneration and expenses of elected officials are subject to the appropriate provincial statutes that govern municipalities. In some provinces, it is left to councils to adopt a resolution or enact a by-law for the payment of annual stipends. The by-law or resolution may specify the manner of payment and the conditions under which an elected official may forfeit all or part of his or her remuneration. Under the Income Tax Act, an elected official can receive up to one-third of the annual stipend in the form of tax-free allowance, providing this money is used to pay for expenses directly related to official duties of the council member. In addition to the fixed stipend, many units provide additional compensation on the basis of the number of meetings that the council members may be required to attend.

Increasingly, it has become the practice to seek the advice of an independent "stipend committee" to recommend to council on remuneration matters. If this is done a few months prior to elections in the last year of Council's term of office, the recommendations will apply to incoming members and will thereby minimize suggestions of conflict of interest on the part of sitting members.

Conflict of Interest

"Conflict of Interest" has always been a thorny and controversial topic in municipal life in Canada. All provinces have attempted to regulate the more blatant expressions of conflict through their general municipal legislation. In Nova Scotia, a separate statute, the Municipal Conflict of Interest Act, came into effect in 1982. This Act sets down rules of procedure to be followed by a council member in declaring a conflict of interest. Likewise the Municipal Elections Act sets out the qualifications a person must meet to be nominated and to serve as a member of Council.

All elected officials and those aspiring to public office should make themselves familiar with legislation governing real and perceived conflict. Each council member or candidate is responsible for determining where they may have a conflict and to act accordingly. While the municipal solicitor or the clerk cannot assume responsibility for advising individual councillors on specific situations, these officials should be consulted on general areas of potential conflict.

Specific disqualification grounds may be spelled out in legislation, but the references deal mostly with pecuniary interests, direct and indirect. Other areas of potential conflict of interest are more difficult to define. It is primarily a matter of living up to the expectations of the community of what is proper and honourable behaviour for an elected representative. The situation has been summarized:[9]

> It is highly desirable that those elected to govern are completely free to arrive at decisions based on their opinions on policy, without being influenced by factors or ulterior motives which would prevent disinterested and unbiased decisions from being made. Public policy requires that in order to ensure purity of administration, any person who participates in the decision-making process should not be in such a position that he might be suspected of being biased. The fundamental rule that a personal interest in a matter disqualifies a member from voting was firmly fixed in the ancient practice of parliamentary bodies. A conflict of interest can simply be defined as any circumstance where the personal interest of the council member in a matter

9 Ian MacF. Rogers, "Conflict of Interest – A Trap for Unwary Politicians", reprinted in *Municipal World* (May 1974), p.114.

before council may prevent him, or appear to prevent him, from giving an unbiased decision with respect to such matter.

At a minimum, legislation requires that a member of council who has an interest in a matter before council must declare such interest, and may be required to withdraw from the chamber while the matter is being dealt with.

Powers of Elected Officials in Relation to Appointed Officials

In a very small one-man business the owner makes all the decisions and may do all the work. As the business grows, the owner may still make all the decisions but may have help in administration of the business.

A corporation is a "fictitious person", unable to make decisions. Therefore, the corporation has a board of directors which makes the corporation's decisions. It may directly engage employees to perform the work, or it may designate a senior staff person to make such hiring decisions.

The situation in a municipal corporation is somewhat comparable to that of a private corporation, with the mayor or warden and councillors the equivalent of a board of directors. The operation of the municipal unit has two distinct elements. The first includes the "matters of policy", which requires the making of decisions. The second is seeing that these decisions are carried out, which is the job of "administration". The dividing line between what is policy and what is administration, however, is often unclear.

Basically, policy decisions are made in council meetings by the elected officials meeting either as members of their councils or as members of various boards and committees established by council. The broad general lines of policies and programs are determined and enacted by the elected officials. Implementing the resulting policies and programs is the responsibility of the appointed officials, who are in fact and in law instructed by the decisions of the elected officials made in council or at committee and board meetings.

As provided in the provincial legislation, councils may choose to designate their senior staff person as the City or Town Manager, or as the Chief Administrative Officer (CAO). Many municipal units, however, continue to operate with the clerk-treasurer designation, even though the demands of the office are very different from what they have been in the past. Regardless of the title, the knowledge, competence, and judgement of the senior staff person will be reflected in the ability of the entire staff group to support council in its service to the community.

Municipal councils are generally responsible for the hiring of appointed municipal officers, although in larger units this responsibility may be shared with the manager or chief administrative officer. Less senior staff appointments may be entirely delegated to the CAO or clerk-treasurer. In most municipalities, formal approval of hirings is required by council or by the appropriate committee or board. In certain instances, such as in the hiring of municipal or town clerks, the appointment carries with it a certain security and tenure of office. When not otherwise specifically provided in legislation, the ordinary principles of the employee-employer relationship govern, and an appointed official may be removed from office only for just cause, or because the contract of employment has terminated, or because the incumbent is no longer required to perform the function for which appointment was made. Where collective agreements govern the employee's relationship to the municipal unit, termination procedures are usually spelled out in some detail.

We will return to a more detailed discussion of the council-administration relationship in Chapter V.

The Functions of the Municipal Solicitor

The municipal solicitor, whether acting for a city, town, village, or other type of municipality, is a professional lawyer retained or employed to give professional advice to the municipal unit. In cities and towns, a municipal solicitor is normally guaranteed certain tenure of office, subject to "good behaviour". This has the advantage that the municipal solicitor has some protection against censure when expressing his or her independent professional advice.

The municipal solicitor is generally responsible for drafting municipal legislation, regulations, and by-laws; examining and giving opinions on municipal documents and contracts; negotiating settlements of claims; participating in labour negotiations; conducting on behalf of the municipality, after proper authority is received, all legal proceedings; attending council, committee, and board meetings and giving advice on procedure and interpretation of documents and statutes; and generally providing the same services to the municipal client as is offered to other clients.

The municipal solicitor is not in any way the lawyer either for individual elected officials, for appointed officials, or for individual ratepayers or groups of ratepayers. He or she acts for the municipal corporation and should not, in discharging his or her duties, risk a conflict of interest by acting for individuals where the municipality may be involved.

In larger municipal units, the position of solicitor is likely a full-time staff position. Elsewhere the duties are filled by a lawyer acting on a part-time basis. In certain cases, it may be appropriate to arrange for special legal counsel to assist in areas requiring more specialized legal knowledge or experience.

The Letter and the Spirit

Most council members do not need to be reminded that the letter of the law does not always govern the spirit in which law is administered. What determines the quality of our democracy is often the degree of vigilance that is exercised in seeing that fairness, compassion and even common sense are used in applying the law.

No one who has lived through the Donald Marshall enquiry can doubt that in the past, there has often been one "law" for the comfortable white majority, and another, more sinister set of rules for members of certain minority groups. The temptation to condemn without due process must be vigorously combatted. The Charter of Rights and Freedoms sets out our national commitment to equality before the law in matters of race, language, colour, religion, sex, age, and mental or physical disabilities. But to translate this commitment into real changes in the way we deal with minorities or the disadvantaged, requires a considerable adjustment in opinions, attitudes, and behaviour. For the municipal councillors a good place to start is in examining hiring policies throughout the workforce, and in ensuring that municipal police departments have active programs to promote good race relations throughout the community.

Those who represent their communities in elected offices have the opportunity and the power through their leadership and example to give substance to the spirit of the law. If this were to be the watchword of politics, the image of the elected politician would be enormously enhanced.

Summary

Canadian governments have developed a strong legal tradition in support of the concept of the "rule of law" and the rights and freedoms of individual citizens. In the Canadian Constitution, the Charter of Rights and Freedoms gives recognition to this concept, making it binding on all levels and all agencies of government.

As a federation of provinces and territories, the Canadian Constitution has sought to define the respective jurisdictions of the Government of Canada and the individual provincial legislatures. The original document setting forth this division of powers, the British North America Act of 1867, has been considerably modified in its apparent intent by judicial interpretations, or as known in legal jargon, by case law. That the Constitution is a living document is often, and sometimes painfully, obvious, since its amendment has been a subject of heated national debate for a very long time.

Although some attempts continue to be made to carve out a constitutional niche that would entrench the right of local governments to exist, these efforts do not appear to be headed for success anytime soon. So, for the foreseeable future, municipal institutions in our Maritime provinces will, in a legal sense, continue to be "creatures of the Province".

This chapter has reviewed the framework of law with respect to municipal government, and has considered the powers of legislation allocated to councils. Some of the legal constraints with respect to conflict of interest, elected-appointed relations, and the role of the municipal solicitor, have also been outlined. The use of regulation as a method of giving effect to political decisions has been discussed.

Finally, the chapter has sounded a caution that the functions of local government do not consist solely in the mechanical application and interpretation of laws or regulations.

Chapter IV

What Does Local Government Do?

Introduction

The question may be asked (and sometimes is) about the basic purpose of local government. In an age when communication is almost instantaneous, when transportation has compressed distances from several days of travel to a matter of hours and minutes, and when increasingly a workplace is in front of a computer screen in a spare room at home, is it really necessary to maintain all the paraphernalia of this very junior level of administration and decision making? Many functions of municipalities only amount to the administration of provincial programs in accordance with provincial policies, standards and instructions. Since their provincial masters mostly treat them as their obedient creatures, why not do away with the fiction of local self-government? Why go through all the bother of municipal elections, the rigmarole of council meetings, the expense of municipal buildings, administrative staff, telephones, computers and faxes, and all the other trappings of political existence? The direct delivery of many provincial services is managed centrally and only occasionally with modest local sub-units of provincial departments.

The abolition of local government is not as bizarre an idea as it may appear at first glance. After all, it happened in New Brunswick in 1967, when the "Equal Opportunities" program did away with all county municipalities. It happened in Prince Edward Island, when a number of suburban municipal units disappeared into the City of Summerside or into the three consolidated municipalities in the Charlottetown area. It happened in Nova Scotia in 1996, when half a dozen formerly autonomous units were folded into the Cape Breton Regional Municipality, or when Dartmouth, Halifax, Bedford, and the Halifax County Municipality became absorbed into the Halifax Regional Municipality. And the process of doing away with local units of government is not confined to the Maritime provinces, as was demonstrated in the forced amalgamation of reluctant municipalities in the Toronto metropolitan area.

The pressures for reductions in the numbers of municipal units has been accompanied by a reduction in the responsibilities of the remaining or successor units. The Equal Opportunities program in New Brunswick included the assumption by the province of all responsibility for education, social services, health, and the administration of justice. These services have also become the exclusive obligation of the Government of Prince Edward Island. In Nova Scotia, the municipal reform agenda has included a "service exchange" program under which the province is to assume full operational responsibility for social services, health and education, and in exchange, policing and local roads are to fall under municipal jurisdiction.[1]

Over time these reforms have constituted major changes in the structure and operations of local government in the Maritime provinces. The changes are not only to the list of municipal services, but also affect how decisions are made by councils, and they have far reaching financial implications for local governments.

The Municipal Menu

We will now turn towards an examination of the responsibilities that currently form the *raison d'être* of local government in the Maritime provinces. These will be considered under four headings:

- Government Services
- Regulatory Services
- Core Municipal Services
- The Agency Role

Government Services

In municipal budgets, expenditures for the operation and maintenance of council offices, the stipends and expenses of council members, and costs of the general administration, are listed under the heading of Government Services. This includes the purposes and the operations of the council and its administration under the sub-headings of *political and legislative activities,* and *administrative services.*

Political and Legislative Activities

The political role of local government may often be obscured by its more visible preoccupation with the delivery of hard services, such as roads, water, garbage disposal, and similar services to the owners of property.

1 These changes have been discussed in Chapter I.

But representing the views of citizens, mediating between conflicting interests in the community, making choices between maintaining minimal tax rates and providing adequate levels of services, determining priorities for the allocation of resources, formulating and passing of resolutions and by-laws giving effect to policies—these are all matters for governmental decision making. How effectively such decisions are made and implemented will largely determine the economic and social health of the community. These are the functional areas of council activities that sometimes are overlooked in the scramble by provincial authorities to amalgamate, to rationalize, and to downplay the roles and responsibilities of their local governments.

Administrative Services

Apart from the legislative role of local government, there is the administrative arm that not only supports the policy work of the council, but which also delivers the managerial and clerical services required to keep the system in operation.

A principal task is to maintain communication with citizens. This includes over-the-counter and telephone queries, handling of correspondence, the circulation of information bulletins, notices, press releases, and providing access to a myriad of information on all aspects of the municipality. It involves preparation of agendas and recording of minutes, the arrangement of public meetings, press conferences, and the welcoming of tourists and other visitors.

The financial side involves keeping of tax records, preparation and mailing of tax billings, collection of taxes, local improvement charges, area rates, parking fees and fines. The finance department also keeps track of all expenditures, preparing tender documents, issuing purchase orders, preparing the payroll for employees, and issuing cheques for expenses and accounts payable.

Regulatory Services

Regulation is a necessary element in human society. In a democracy, the ideal is to encourage personal behaviour that reduces the need for formal rules as much as possible. But it is obvious that total absence of regulation is neither possible nor desirable. On an individual basis, many things are not tolerated for reasons of safety, health, social fairness or even ordinary convenience. We do not accept violence of one person against another, we have rules about sanitation, about smoking in public places, about vandalism, about speed limits, parking, and other traffic infractions.

We have regulations to protect the environment, to keep domestic animals from running wild, to conserve natural resources such as fish, wild animals, birds and endangered plants. We have rules about when tax payments are made, about respect for the property of others, for discouraging litter and for the preservation of a peaceful community.

Regulation pervades many aspects of municipal operations. Elections for council are governed by procedures to guarantee a secret ballot and reduce the possibility of error or even fraud. Council operates with rules of order to expedite its deliberations. Services are delivered with a good deal of regulatory detail. Transportation is a particularly obvious example, with rules of the road, parking restrictions, licencing, and vehicle inspections by municipal police. Garbage disposal, with the recent emphasis on recycling, has a new set of rules. Water supplies originate in protected watersheds, and certain substances are banned from disposal in sanitary sewage systems. Recreation programs are governed by a variety of rules and many activities are designed to instill a sense of fairness and responsibility.

It is easy to see that without such restraints on human thoughtlessness, our society would soon become intolerable.

Perhaps the most visible of municipal regulatory functions relates to municipal planning activities. Setting out policies to guide future development, laying out the land use by-law, determining the levels of each of the municipal services needed to accommodate anticipated growth in both the commercial and residential sectors, and ensuring that preparations for growth occur in a timely manner, are part of both the governing and the regulatory responsibility. Planning is a separate topic and will be discussed more fully in Chapter VIII.

Core Municipal Services

During discussions on municipal reform, a major question often deals with the most appropriate allocation of service responsibilities between the provincial and the local levels. This has led to attempts to define classes of services in order to help decide who should do what. One school of thought distinguishes between "services to people" and "services to property". Social services or education are offered as examples of services that are directed specifically to individuals and therefore ought to belong in the provincial domain. On the other hand, water supply, sewage disposal, road maintenance, and garbage removal are more directly related to property needs and therefore should be provided by the municipalities. A related approach uses the terms general services and local services and arrives at a similar allocation.

A different way of looking at services is to consider them under three headings: active services provided directly to people; passive services, which includes standby services that are available when needed; and regulatory services, which include rules and regulations that help to ensure a safe, healthy and attractive community. While classifications are sometimes useful in thinking about what local governments are for, we should not lose sight of the fact that in our system of government, all services are provided for people. In any case, there is now a fairly comparable list of municipally delivered services in each of the three Maritime provinces. Instead of choosing any one classification method, we will consider the core services that are most often part of the municipal agenda in this region.

Transportation Services

Under Transportation Services, there are three sub-headings: Municipal Roads; Parking; and Public Transit.

Municipal Roads

While the Maritime provinces construct and maintain their provincial highway networks, the servicing of roads in cities and towns is generally a municipal responsibility. Streets and roads in residential areas are normally installed by the developer during the subdivision process, but upon completion their upkeep becomes a municipal matter. Until recently, rural roads of all types in Nova Scotia were under provincial jurisdiction, but the 1996 program of service exchange envisaged that residential road maintenance would be transferred to the rural municipalities, although transitional arrangements are still being worked out.

Municipal road services include a broad range of activities: construction, repair and maintenance of municipal streets and roads, bridges and sidewalks, and during the winter season, salting, sanding, and snow removal; street lighting; traffic signs and signals; and cross-walk patrols.

For their part, the provinces generally are responsible for provincial and interprovincial highways; bridges and roads in unorganized areas, as well as major arterial roads which run through organized areas.

Parking

In the cities and towns, parking offers a significant challenge. Much of the decline of urban downtown areas can be traced to our automobile culture. Traditional main street shopping has moved to suburban plazas, malls and industrial parks, primarily for traffic and parking reasons. The demand for parking close to offices and stores has placed pressures on the urban land resource, thus creating a further incentive for the flight to the suburbs. Municipal councils have sometimes attempted to counteract this trend through the provision of public parking lots, the installation of parking meters and hefty fines to discourage long-term street parking, as well as enacting building codes designed to force new construction to include space for off-street parking. None of these measures has proven to be spectacularly successful in modifying the impact of the automobile.

Public Transit

In theory, the provision of urban transit systems suggests a possible response to the problems of our automobile culture. Offering a low cost, convenient alternative to the automobile, buses, and other mass transportation modes should make it possible to preserve some part of our traditional urban cores. Few municipal councils in Canada's cities, however, have found ways to offer a level playing field for mass transit. The automobile is heavily subsidized by the huge public investments in highways, urban expressways, and the massive land areas required for our networks of city and town streets to serve both residential and commercial properties. In most urban areas, buses join the congestion of private cars with a consequent loss of any advantages in cost, time saving or convenience.

The result has been that urban transit in many communities has become a service used mostly by persons on low incomes for whom an automobile is an unattainable luxury. The response of many councils has been as predictable as it has been regrettable: let the service pay for itself with higher fares. As more users are forced to abandon the system, eventually closing it will rid the municipality of another expensive subsidy!

Environmental Services

This service category includes sewer and water services as well as the collection and disposal of solid waste.

Water and Sewage

Water and sewage services are concerned with providing safe drinking water and handling sewer effluents. In larger urban areas, it may also include storm sewer installations in connection with local road networks.

In the cities and towns and in urban areas of rural municipalities, water supply and sewage collection systems are municipal responsibilities. In the past, both the provincial and federal governments have provided substantial capital grants for the construction of such facilities. Where local geography permits, the system may be jointly owned and operated by two or more adjoining municipalities under some form of regional authority, with each municipality sharing in the costs based on a formula such as property assessment, flow rate or some other combination.

As environmental controls become increasingly demanding, urban municipal governments face sharply increased costs in meeting higher minimum standards for water and sewage facilities. In many municipalities, it is mandatory that developers pay for installation of lateral water and waste pipes in new subdivisions. The use of metered water rates allows recovery of municipal costs.

Solid Waste

Collection and disposal of residential and commercial garbage is generally a municipal responsibility. With the arrival of recycling and composting, this service has become increasingly complex. Most municipalities have in the past managed their own waste disposal, but there is an increasing trend towards regional co-operation in the handling of recyclables and the operation of composting and landfill facilities. The collection may be carried out by municipal works departments or may be contracted out to private operators through a tendering process.

The location of landfill sites is often a highly charged emotional issue in many communities. Provinces are adopting increasingly higher standards and generally require environmental assessment of new sites. Environmental and community groups have become vocal in their opposition to poorly planned or sited locations. Although such interventions have made it more difficult and expensive to find solutions, the net effect has been to raise public awareness of the enormous environmental damage that may result from improper waste handling. The success of programs of recycling and the composting of organic wastes owes much to this increased public vigilance.

Recreation and Culture

In combination, these services enhance the well-being of residents and their quality of life. These municipal services are concerned with operation and maintenance of physical facilities such as parks, playgrounds, sports fields, swimming pools, skating rinks and arenas, museums and historic sites. On the program side, municipal recreation departments generally initiate and organize a variety of recreational activities, and provide organizational and financial assistance to community volunteer groups such as sports bodies, cultural societies, and clubs.

Social Assistance

In the early days of Canadian municipal administration, social welfare service was a central concern for local governments. Care of the indigent and mentally disturbed in community "poor houses" was often financed by a separate property tax levy. With greater emphasis on social services that emerged from the Great Depression and following World War II, the federal and provincial governments became major contributors to the rising costs, and municipal involvement dwindled. In both Prince Edward Island and New Brunswick, the respective provinces have for some years assumed full responsibility. Under the Nova Scotia Service Exchange Program, the province in 1996 took over responsibilities that had previously fallen to the municipal level, although local councils are still required to contribute a transitional levy to the province.

Housing

Government housing services provide for housing or housing assistance to low income earners, the elderly, and the disabled. These activities may include: subsidized rental housing, public housing projects, co-op housing, seniors' apartments, and mortgage assistance programs.

This field is dominated by the two senior levels of governments through provincial housing initiatives and Canada Mortgage and Housing Corporation (CMHC) programs. When municipalities are involved, it is usually in the form of assisted-cost housing or senior citizen housing. They may also be participants in co-sponsored programs involving all three government levels. Such co-sponsored housing projects may be seen in a number of urban municipalities in the region.

For the most part, subsidies extended by senior governments tend to reduce the need for municipal funding participation. Controversy surrounding public housing occurs in the location and design of the proposed developments. The most common reaction to locating a subsidized housing project in an existing neighbourhood is the NIMBY response - Not In My Back Yard.

As part of the housing agenda, many provincial and municipal governments operate land-banking programs to provide an inventory of building sites for future housing and commercial development.

Education

Education is a provincial responsibility in Prince Edward Island and New Brunswick. In those provinces, local school boards or school parent committees are essentially advisory to provincial education departments. For several decades there has been no municipal involvement in education matters in these provinces.

In Nova Scotia, municipal participation in education policy making has for most purposes disappeared. At the same time, however, all municipalities are required to collect a provincial property tax earmarked for education and levied at an uniform rate throughout the province. A major complaint of municipal councillors is that this levy severely restricts their own revenue raising ability and that it violates the principle that the taxing authority should be directly accountable to the taxpayer.

In the case of the Halifax Regional Municipality (HRM), taxpayers in the former cities of Halifax and Dartmouth have historically paid an additional property tax rate to enable their own school boards to finance extra school programs such as enhanced physical education and music. This practice has been continued under the amalgamated system, and other Community Councils within the HRM have the option of adding a similar levy for the benefit of their local schools.

Protective Services

Fire and police protection are basic municipal services in urban areas. In rural areas, policing is generally a provincial responsibility. Fire protection is provided by municipal or volunteer departments. Building inspection is usually carried out by municipal inspectors.

Police Protection

Policing is intended to provide protection for people against assault, theft, property damage, and other forms of criminal activity. In some communities, the police service is evolving into a more activist role through the concept of community policing. An example is the leadership by police in helping young people cope with stresses of urban living, which has proven effective in reducing problems of vandalism, drug abuse, and confrontations with racial or ethnic overtones. The daily activities of an activist police department will cover a spectrum of services such as regular and special patrols, community relations and safety education, emergency responses, traffic control, apprehension of offenders, attendance at special events, serving warrants, vehicle documents examination, accident and offences reports, and services at Court sessions.

Across Canada, provincial governments are responsible for policing in unorganized territories and in the smaller organized communities. This responsibility is frequently carried out by provincial police forces or by contract with the Royal Canadian Mounted Police. In the Maritime provinces, regional municipalities, cities and towns are all required to provide their own police services. Some provinces provide municipalities with a per capita or per household police grant to help finance a mandated level of police service. In Nova Scotia, the 1996 Service Exchange program served notice that rural municipalities would be required to assume the policing function. In some cases it merely means that the RCMP continue to provide the service, but the municipal unit will have to take over costs associated with the service.

In some parts of Canada, provincial governments have assigned to their municipalities responsibility for maintaining courthouses and providing overnight lockups. Out of financial necessity, neighbouring municipalities in Nova Scotia have, in the past, often combined resources to construct and maintain correctional facilities. As the lockup is seen as the front end of the provincial correctional process, the operation of these facilities has now been assumed by the province, but municipalities continue to be responsible for part of the costs.

Fire Protection

In every province, fire protection is a local responsibility. In general, the provincial share of this responsibility is borne by the office of the provincial fire marshall, who sets service standards, provides technical assistance to local fire departments, and conducts complex investigations as required.

In regional municipalities and cities of the Maritime provinces, fire departments are an integral part of municipal organization. Staff are full-time professionals, sometimes supported by auxiliary volunteer corps. In smaller towns and in rural areas, protection is provided by volunteer fire companies supported by annual grants and by various fund raising activities.

To the general public, fire departments provide protection for structures, contents of structures and the people who live, work or do business in those structures. Fire prevention inspections and education are an important part of their functions. Increasingly fire departments also provide medical emergency response and first aid, traffic and other accident rescue operations, water sport rescues and drowning resuscitation. In smaller towns and rural communities, the fire department serves as a focal point for many community social functions and volunteer activities.

Overall, municipal fire protection services will, in addition to fire call responses, include fire prevention inspection services, investigations for fire cause, auxiliary services such as rescues, attendance at highway and industrial accidents, emergency/disaster planning, medical emergency first aid, and public education programs.

The Agency Role

To a large extent, municipalities are important instruments of both federal and provincial policy. As we have seen in Chapter I, under the Canadian Constitution the federal government has no direct authority over the local level, but the power of the purse often speaks far more effectively than any clause enshrined in the Constitution. Thus housing policies exercised through Canada Mortgage and Housing Corporation (CMHC) continue to shape the form and direction of urban development in many communities, the federal infrastructure program has been a powerful instrument in job creation objectives, and "grants-in-lieu" of taxes on federal Crown properties are an important component in many municipal budgets. Such levers are highly effective in encouraging municipal units to react positively to underlying federal aims.

The provincial level has a more direct influence on local government actions. The Constitution is unequivocal in defining the legal subservience of municipal institutions to provinces. This basic power relationship is reinforced by the system of conditional grants which makes it financially advantageous to accept provincial programs and priorities. Every shared cost program is an expression of this reality. During the most acute period of provincial fiscal restraint, municipal payrolls were subject to the same fiscal squeeze imposed on provincial government employees. The wave of municipal amalgamations unilaterally imposed by provincial cabinets in recent years further emphasizes the reality of the power relationship.

While there are many similarities among the Maritime provinces in the functions of their local governments, Nova Scotia differs markedly from New Brunswick and Prince Edward Island in its taxation system. In the latter two, property tax is levied both by individual municipal units as well as by the province, but collection of the combined tax receivables is carried out by the province. Thus, the provincial revenue department acts as agent/tax collector for the municipal units.

In contrast, the government of Nova Scotia levies a fixed property tax rate in support of education, and requires the municipal units to include this rate with their own tax billing. Likewise, the province requires as a transitional measure that municipalities make a municipal contribution to provincial expenditures on social services. In these cases, the role of the municipal units is the ultimate in agency responsibility—they act as tax collectors for the province.

What Else Should Local Government Do?

There are people, including some in public life, who think that local councils should do nothing that is not absolutely necessary for a minimum of basic services. This "minimalist" school would expect council decision-making to deal with little more serious than the time for switching street lights on and off.

The authors of this book do not share this philosophy. We do not believe that local governments should be viewed entirely as delivery agents or as administrative conveniences for provincially-constructed programs. We believe that local government is for local choice and that differences in choices made between municipal communities is not only acceptable, but often desirable. Each council needs to have the authority to act as a deliberative body and to truly engage in governing. A primary responsibility of local councils is to make decisions about the nature and level of services that best meet the needs of their citizens, but council members should also find time to identify community issues, seek solutions and explore opportunities for the community to come to grips with its problems. Activities of these types can best be described under the term *community economic development*, or CED.

Community Economic Development

Community economic development (CED), as used herein, may be defined as a process concerned with improving the quality of life for members of a particular community. In this sense, it includes social as well as economic development. This broader definition takes the concept well beyond obvious topics such as business development, employment increase and income growth. To these it adds matters such as affordable housing, quality health care, recreation opportunities, and clean air and water. The word "development" implies an active process that involves the community in developing goals, engaging in planning activities, and evaluating resulting action and outcomes.

The whole area of community economic development is where local government can gain the experience and provide the leadership necessary for real social and economic progress. There are various possibilities in most communities. These could include building upon existing capabilities within the municipal organization, or within community organizations such as Boards of Trade, professional groups, co-operative societies, credit unions, and trade union locals; co-operating with neighbouring communities in a joint or regional authority; or even establishing an entirely new authority to co-ordinate and support other available forces.

Once the organizational form is established, the second step is to ensure that the necessary resources are in place. Financial resources are of course important, but priority initially should be placed on securing the best possible human resources. Energetic, innovative and dedicated leadership able to work effectively with other community resources is a key ingredient.

The third step is to identify the needs the strategy is to satisfy. In other words, what are the goals and objectives that are important, and what are the community values that are worth preserving? Industrial development may be desirable from an economic point of view, but what if it leads to unacceptable levels of congestion or pollution? Tourism development may seem beneficial but what if increasing attractiveness of the area causes land prices to escalate, bringing increased assessment to existing homeowners and perhaps placing property ownership beyond the reach of the local population? The key is for each community to identify its own goals and to avoid the temptation to arrive at quick or convenient conclusions that may penalize some group of residents or interfere with the goals of another community.

The process of developing community goals should be inclusive. There should be reasonable opportunity for community leaders, businesses, groups and individuals to participate in the process. This approach will be of value in two respects. First, it may generate valuable insight into the community, and second, it will help to establish community "buy-in" into the process and create a sense of ownership in its successful implementation. For this to succeed, a special effort will be needed to ensure that those who are normally under-represented or who lack the confidence or resources to effectively participate are enabled to have their views given legitimacy and to have them reflected in final decisions.

A fourth step is to develop an understanding of the economic base of the community. Since data collection and analysis will be an important element of the process, this may be the point at which a community will require specialized help. Such understanding will significantly improve the chance for success of the strategy by helping to identify the community's competitive advantages in the market place and thereby enable the community to target potential investment.

The fifth step in the process is to identify the community's strengths and weaknesses. This will require frank and critical self-examination. Identifying strengths is an important ingredient in any marketing of the community, but it is also essential to find weaknesses that need to be addressed. This will also include a reasonable assessment of the available financial, human and even political resources. A strategy should contemplate initiatives which are realistic in terms of the resources available. These are all factors in developing a database that will provide invaluable assistance in decision making.

In each of these steps, it is essential to maintain a consistent focus throughout the process. Communities should strive to maintain some degree of diversification in the economic base. Putting all of the "eggs in one basket" may lead to disaster, as has happened all too often in communities whose prosperity depended on a single industry or type of industry. On the other hand, a strategy should not seek unrealistic goals that may go beyond the available resources. Additionally, the temptation to "jump on the bandwagon" of current fads should be resisted. An example of such blunders has been the blind rush by many municipality's to develop industrial parks which had little basis for their creation.

The final step in strategic planning is an ongoing process of evaluation and refinement. The best laid plans often go awry because the world has unfolded in ways that could not have been predicted by the original planners. Learning from experience and adaptation to circumstance can turn a potential misfortune into future wisdom.

The Changing Nature of Government

The traditional role of government as a unique or sole provider of services is being challenged on many sides. In response, governments are increasingly beginning to view their primary roles as helping to define, shape, meet and protect the public interest in a variety of ways. This mandate may mean that services are organized and delivered in new and different ways. In some types of services, the need will continue to require a direct and dominant role for government. In other cases, however, governments may decide that the public interest may be more efficiently met through some other way. This may be achieved by passing some particular service responsibility on to the private sector, or sharing delivery through co-operative arrangements with other governments, independent commissions or non-profit organizations. Many examples of this devolution have occurred in the last decades.

At the federal level, a number of Crown corporations have been turned into private corporations, such as Petro Canada, Air Canada, and Canadian National Railways. Others have been sold outright, such as the Connaught Laboratories complex of pharmaceutical manufacturers, which was sold to a French multinational concern. The National Harbours Board is in the process of divesting itself of Canadian ports. Airports are being turned over to local non-profit authorities. The federal air traffic control system has been turned over to a private operator.

At the provincial level, the same process is underway in many provinces. In the Maritimes, toll roads are recent examples, as is the Confederation bridge connecting Prince Edward Island to New Brunswick. Gambling casinos are described as "joint ventures" between a provincial authority and a private operator. In Nova Scotia, schools are being built as "private partnering" ventures, with capital costs being provided through by private corporations.

Municipalities have joined in this movement. Where once municipal governments believed that all local programs and services needed to be organized and delivered, exclusively, by the municipal staff, there is growing recognition and appreciation of the value of developing strong partnerships including partnerships with community-based organizations. In many communities, the collection of garbage has been turned over to private contractors. Road and street maintenance is often carried out as a combination of public works and contracting out. On the other hand, intermunicipal co-operation has been growing in areas such as recycling and land fill operations.

The practical consequence for governments has been to place increased emphasis on policy analysis, policy development and program evaluation. With these tools, governments are able to better understand the public interest and ensure that programs, irrespective of the delivery system, are meeting the public need. Undoubtedly the economic climate has been an important ingredient in this new way of conducting government business, but there is an interesting coincidence of interests emerging. Governments are exploring, even experimenting, with creative and innovative ways of meeting the public need, which implies more direct public involvement. Community-based organizations have longed for the opportunity to be recognized as an important part of any development strategy.

Municipalities are well aware of the value of working with community-based groups in areas such as recreation and fire services. In these examples, the municipality benefits from the energy, ingenuity and community spirit of highly motivated volunteers. Here the role of local government is mainly one of providing funding by means of grants, but such expenditures are invariably far less than the value that volunteers contribute in service to the community. This principle can be extended to a variety of other service areas, such as community economic development, tourism promotion and operation of facilities such as swimming pools, arenas and playgrounds. Even in areas not directly related to municipal responsibilities, councils can assist by showing official support and offering seed money for new initiatives. Examples abound. In the case of the work of the Canadian Mental Health Association, many municipalities have added impetus to programs of life skills, job entry training, and social support programming. With the health agencies such as the Canadian Cancer Society, the Heart and Stroke Foundation, the Lung Association, and local units of the Canadian Medical Association, many municipalities have assisted in campaigns to reduce tobacco smoke health hazards through by-laws restricting smoking in public places. Seniors' clubs have been assisted by providing programming in municipally-owned facilities. The list of innovative approaches by municipal councils is practically endless, but in all cases, a little support, financial and otherwise, can go a long way in fostering civic pride while improving the quality of life in the community.

As we enter a new millennium, municipalities will need, increasingly, to see themselves in these broader roles as partners, facilitators, advisors, supporters and funders. By helping to build a stronger network of volunteer organizations and community-oriented private sector partnerships, the local government council will be able to change its image from one of rowing the municipal ship to one of steering it. For some councillors and administrators, these new roles will be unfamiliar and will require new vision and new skills. The effort to change may be demanding, but ultimately will be worth it.

Summary

In this chapter, we have broadly described some of the traditional functions of local government and how these functions have changed, and continue to change, over time. Since the service responsibilities of municipal units in the Maritime provinces are in an almost constant state of flux, our descriptions should be recognized as being merely a snapshot taken within the narrow time period when this volume was being prepared.

Under the heading of Government Services, we have briefly looked at how, and to what extent, councils perform a basic political or governance role as distinct from the administrative functions that go with the operation of municipal offices. Under the heading of Regulatory Services, we emphasize how rules and regulations are necessary elements for any safe, peaceful and attractive community. Core Municipal Services include all of the typical municipal housekeeping activities that are essential for a functioning society in the Maritime provinces. Under The Agency Role section, we deal with obligations that are imposed on municipalities by each of the provinces. These are generally areas in which the local council have little or no decision-making involvement but where they are expected to deliver or administer tasks set for them by their provincial masters.

In the final section on what else municipalities should be doing, we have discussed some of the recent pressures for local government to take a more proactive role in the broader governance process.

Chapter V

Municipal Decision Making

Introduction

The purpose of this chapter is to provide the reader with an overview of decision making in municipal government. The chapter is organized under the following major headings: the players, the structures, the processes and relationships.

As we learned in Chapter III, municipalities are incorporated bodies whose powers are restricted to matters specifically delegated to them by their provincial governments. As such we often hear the expression that municipalities are "creatures" of the province. It is true that they have no independent status and can be created, amended or dissolved at the will of the provincial legislature. It is this legal relationship, along with the fiscal relationship outlined in Chapter VII, that provided the theme for a paper commissioned a few years ago by the Federation of Canadian Municipalities with the title "Puppets on a Shoestring".[1] The title reflects the frustration that municipalities have long felt about how they are perceived and treated by their provincial governments.

This theme, which has become a dominant part of provincial-municipal relationships, will make its appearance in a number of places in this chapter. It will become particularly important in the discussion of the structures of municipal government in relation to the processes of municipal governance.

The Players

The Municipal Council

A council, most often, is comprised of elected councillors and a mayor. In rural municipalities of Nova Scotia the chairperson is called "Warden"

1 *Puppets on a Shoestring*. Ottawa: Federation of Canadian Municipalities, 1976.

when the incumbent is elected from among regular council members. In community municipalities in Prince Edward Island the title is simply chairman.

The municipal council is the governing body of all municipal units and as such is responsible for exercising powers and duties delegated by the province. On the procedural side, provincial legislation usually contains provisions for matters such as numbers of members of council, election procedures and requirements for frequency of meetings. More will be said later on the methods of municipal elections and their implications, but the reader may wish to consult the specific legislation governing these matters in each of the three provinces. In Appendix B is a list of the main pieces of legislation which deal with municipalities, their structure, methods of election, and powers.

Basis for Municipal Elections

Depending on the particular practices in each province, municipal councils are elected in different ways. The first method is by direct election based upon wards or districts. Here the municipality is divided into appropriate subdivisions usually on the basis of criteria such as size and population. After the announced date for nominations has passed, an election is held in each ward or district where there is a contest. Where only one candidate for a seat has been nominated, that candidate is acclaimed. Where legislation calls for a mayor, he or she is elected at large by all voters in the municipality.

The second method is by direct election without ward or districts. In this case all candidates run on the "at large" basis. Here votes are cast for all the nominated candidates by all eligible voters of the municipality. The available seats on council are allocated to the candidates receiving the highest number of votes. For example, if a council is comprised of six councillors, the six candidates with the largest vote count would be declared elected.

There are pros and cons to each method. Some argue that the ward system is inherently more democratic in assuring that each area of the municipality has a designated council member to represent its interests. Others would argue that the ward system encourages councillors to bring narrow, parochial issues to the council table at the expense of broader municipal matters. The latter group therefore favours the "at large" system in the belief that it encourages councillors to think of the municipality as a whole, thereby downplaying competition and bickering between different areas. On the other hand, running a campaign where all citizens of the municipality must be approached usually means that the election will be more expensive, thereby discouraging non-wealthy candidates from offering. Lastly there is the question of which system offers greater access, by citizens, to their elected representatives.

Where the community is small and relatively homogeneous there is some appeal to the "at large"system. On a practical level, it is not always easy to find candidates to run for municipal office and it may be easier to run a single contested municipal-wide election than to ensure that each individual ward is contested. However, where a municipality is heterogeneous by virtue of history, culture, race, and ethnicity, then there is cause for concern with the "at large" system. The concern is that not all of these interests will be represented and therefore heard at the municipal council and given appropriate consideration and reflected in municipal policy.

The pros and cons of *ward* versus *at large* elections are undoubtedly reflected in the "hybrid" approach adopted by the municipality of Riverview, New Brunswick. Here four councillors are elected by wards, with three at large. Counting the mayor, who is elected at large, the two systems of representation are thus equally depicted in this compromise.

The third type of municipal representation is by indirect election. This is most common in provinces having two-tier municipal government and where the lower tier appoints members to the upper tier. A different example is found in the rural municipalities of Nova Scotia where the warden is elected by fellow councillors from among their own number. This system may disappear in the future if recommendations are adopted to replace all wardens by mayors.

The Community Council

The concept of a community council was first advanced in a study undertaken by the authors on behalf of the former Halifax County Municipality.[2] It was developed in the search of ways of responding to the needs of rapidly developing urban communities within a largely rural municipality. The study sought to balance the need for overall administrative efficiency with local demands for more access to the way decisions were made on matters affecting urban areas. By delegating councillors from urbanized districts within the County to serve as a Community Council, and giving them authority to deal with matters of primarily local concern, this mechanism satisfied the demand for more community control. It did so without incurring the costs associated with a separate municipal entity. In practice community councils have shown themselves

2 Kell Antoft and Jack Novack. *Urban Areas Study. Study for the Municipality of the County of Halifax.* Halifax: Henson College, June 1987.

to be flexible in response to local circumstance and adaptive to changing needs.

Community councils are up and running in the Halifax Regional Municipality and were provided for in legislation which established the Cape Breton Regional Municipality. With Nova Scotia provincial policy continuing to encourage municipal amalgamation, community councils provide one of the few avenues for retaining community identity through a local deliberative body.

The Municipal Staff

Staff is made up of the appointed officials and support personnel in the municipal organization. Size of the staff group can vary greatly according to the size of the municipal unit, the services it delivers and its financial capacity. The smallest village may have only one or two staff persons while the larger cities and regional municipalities may have staff in the thousands. Senior staff in smaller municipalities tend to be generalists often responsible for a variety of functions, while larger municipalities can afford to employ individuals with more specialized skills and experience.

In the early history of local government in the Maritime provinces, municipal staff were usually drawn from the local community and often lacked formal qualifications. Today, with wider educational opportunities and greater mobility, it is not uncommon for senior municipal officials to seek out and accept positions in other parts of the province, region or country as a means of enhancing their careers. Increasingly such individuals possess higher educational qualifications and continue to pursue opportunities for further professional development.

An important role of senior staff is to provide policy advice to council, and when decisions are made, to carry out the will of council as expressed through by-laws, resolutions and directives. While the professional training, experience and knowledge of the administrative staff are essential inputs into the decision-making process, it is council, ultimately, that has the decision-making responsibility.

It is an inherent reality of local government that staff often must work under heavy pressure. The notion of the under-worked, over-paid civil servant just does not apply to the vast majority of municipal employees in the Maritime provinces. This is particularly true of the senior administrative staff who frequently must spend long hours in preparing background documents and attending a constant succession of evening meetings of council and its committees, all while keeping up with their regular workday responsibilities.

Statutory Officers

Certain staff positions in a municipality are provided for in specific provincial legislation. In these situations, the duties of the office defined by statute may not be eliminated or amended by the municipal administration or the municipal council. As a consequence, there are significant limitations on the ability of council as well as other senior staff to direct the work of officers such as the municipal clerk, the municipal treasurer, or the development officer. This limitation is not always understood by citizens nor by individual councillors and accordingly may sometimes give rise to frustration and even conflict.

The Provincial Departments Responsible for Municipal Affairs

In each province there is a department responsible for municipal affairs. At the time of writing, in New Brunswick the department is termed *Municipalities and Housing*; in Prince Edward Island it is the *Department of Community Affairs and Attorney General* and in Nova Scotia it is called *Housing and Municipal Affairs*. During the normal course of cabinet shuffles and departmental reorganizations, the name of every department is subject to change without notice!

By whatever name, these departments play a number of roles. They provide advice and assistance to municipal units. In Nova Scotia and New Brunswick the departments provide this advice and assistance through departmental field staff with job titles such as "Municipal Advisor" and "Municipal Service Representative" respectively. In Prince Edward Island, because of its size a single departmental person is given this responsibility. In all three provinces, departments collect and publish annual statistics on all municipalities, including data on population, assessment, tax rates, municipal expenditures and budgets, and other useful information. The departments serve as windows between the municipal units and their provincial governments, at the same time providing policy advice to the Cabinet on municipal matters. Lastly, the departments generally oversee the affairs of municipal government and in some provinces, screen for approval municipal by-laws and municipal budgets.

As noted earlier, the day of untrained senior municipal staff has mostly disappeared in the Maritime provinces. Most municipalities now employ individuals with first rate professional qualifications and experience. It may, therefore, be no surprise that many, including most municipal officials and some provincial officials, would now challenge the traditional view of a "parental role" as being descriptive of departments responsible for municipal affairs. So as municipalities undergo changes leading to greater sophistication, it is inevitable that the relationship with their provincial counterparts must undergo change as well. Organizationally the provincial trend has been to add to or combine other functions with departments responsible for municipal affairs. This might suggest a narrower and more focused role for these departments in the future.

Special Purpose Bodies

Special purpose bodies have been formed to direct, co-ordinate and/or administer a particular service or regulate an activity. At the municipal level, these include such bodies as planning and industrial commissions, municipal utilities, library and parks boards, and housing authorities.[3] Their common characteristic is their establishment either by municipal by-law or provincial statute. They are usually controlled by separate boards of directors, and though they have no direct taxing authority, they receive a significant amount of their financial support from the local governments they have been set up to serve.

Local Government Structures

In examining the internal decision-making structures of municipalities and other local government bodies, it is evident that there are a number of different models. While one provincial government looks very much like that of any other province, such is not the case with local governmental units. To simplify the discussion, three different decision-making structures for local government in the Maritime region may be described. Understanding how these structures operate and their essential differences is an important first step in developing an appreciation for the relationship between the players.

Council-Committee System

The council-committee system, or more accurately the council-standing committee system, has over the years been a familiar organizational form in many municipalities in the Maritime provinces. In recent years, however, there has been some move away from this model, although many rural municipalities still prefer it.

3 School boards were at one time closely linked to municipal governments, but in recent years this link has been severed.

Council-Committee System

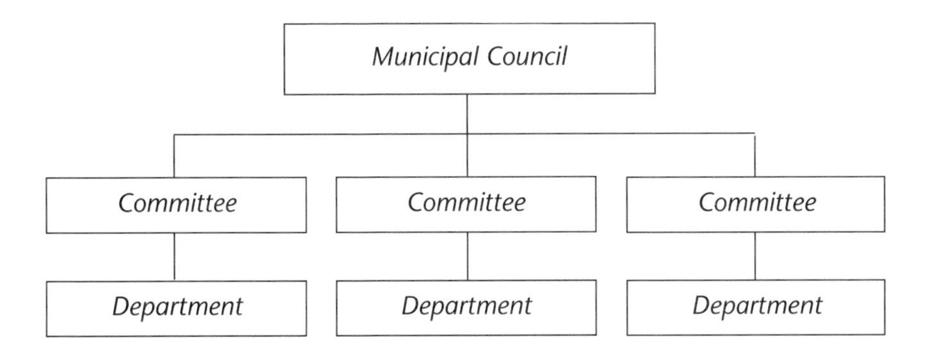

In the council-standing committee system, councillors sit not only as members of municipal council but are selected to serve on one or more of the committees. Some of the more common of these include: Finance; Planning; Recreation; Public Works; and Administration. The exact nature and number of standing committees is a matter for each municipal government to determine, while the frequency of meetings is usually left for committee members to decide.

Much of the business of council is referred to the appropriate standing committee for review and recommendation to full council. These committees perform several functions: they provide policy advice and direction to the municipal council and they provide supervision and direction to a municipal department. The policy role is more typical of larger municipal units while the supervisory role is commonplace in smaller ones. Differences are more in degree than in kind, since committees perform each role to a lesser or greater degree. In the final analysis the committee system is intended to expedite the decision-making process. Whether it helps or hinders varies from one council to the next or from one issue to another.

There are a number of overall advantages in the standing committee system. First, it allows and even encourages detailed examination and consideration before a recommendation is put forward to council. Committees are often better positioned and have more time to seek out citizen and expert advice needed to improve the quality of recommendations to council. Second, the committee system allows councillors to develop detailed knowledge on particular issues and technical matters. Third, committees help to spread the workload of council and thereby relieve staff of what is often their most time-consuming administrative responsibilities, a helpful advantage in smaller municipal units with few staff members. And fourth, the more relaxed and informal tone of a committee assists the deliberative process.

The council-standing committee system is not without its critics. First, it is argued that it tends to fragment decision making by discussing issues on a departmental basis, thereby losing a wider perspective. The recreation committee, for example, might devote considerable energy to decide on the hours of operation of the municipal pool but would tend to spend less time on issues of vandalism or youth unemployment. Such issues likely transcend the particular focus of a single department and often require the efforts, skills and possibly partnership of a variety of individuals and organizations.

Second and related to the first, is a tendency for municipal politicians to misinterpret or confuse their roles as policy makers. Involvement in the management of a municipal department may provide some assistance to the staff but it not the primary function of a municipal politician or likely the reason they were voted into office.

Third, there is the tendency of professional staff to defer to politicians on matters which ought to be part of their regular responsibilities and for which they are paid to exercise judgement. Moreover, the professional staff will often be required to spend too much time organizing committee meetings with all its attendant activity, at the expense of looking after the administration of their departments.

Fourth, discussions conducted at the committee level are often repeated in full at council. As a consequence, the committees' activities contribute to increasing the time and workload of councillors. This can be a serious problem for many council members, who must also attend to their regular employment. It is a common occurrence to have councillors complain that they had grossly underestimated the time needed to discharge their council responsibilities and will cite time as a reason for not re-offering.

Committees which oversee the work of a particular department usually require that the departmental director or other senior member of that department be in attendance. For committees with broad responsibilities, such as an Administrative Committee, the burden often falls on the Chief Administrative Officer or the Municipal Clerk. Such demands on the time of staff, particularly when evening meetings are required, place heavy claims on these individual's time with resulting loss of working efficiency.

Committee of the Whole

To meet some of the objections of the counci-committee system, a number of municipalities have moved to the system of the "Committee of the Whole". In effect, this system involves the folding of most standing committees into a single committee, with all councillors attending its meetings. It encourages every council member to become familiar with most broad aspects of the municipality, and allows much of council's work to be conducted in a more informal manner with a wider range of debate. For some councils, it is also used as a method of meeting behind closed doors to avoid premature release of pending decisions or ongoing discussions on sensitive subjects. As with any committee of council, decisions to be taken must be brought before regular council meetings, which, by law, are required to be open to public attendance and scrutiny.

Council-Manager System

In the earlier days of municipal government in the Canadian provinces, service demands were few and the revenue needs were correspondingly

Council-Manager System

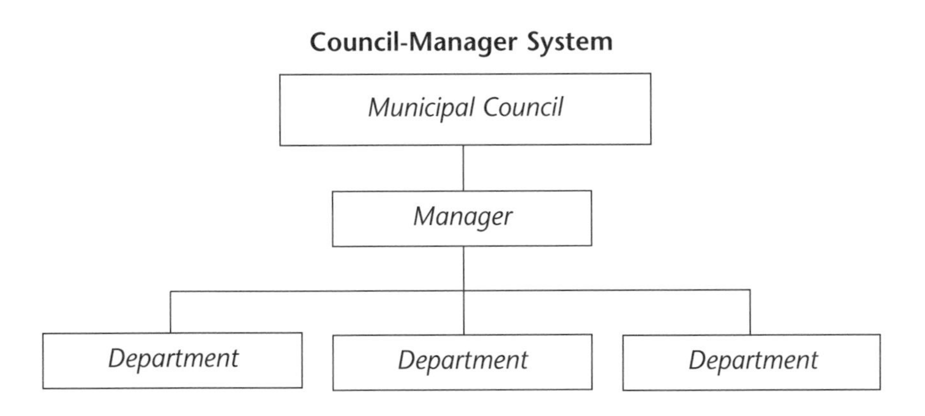

modest. Most of the office work was clerical and relatively simple. Duties could be carried out by individuals without highly specialized skills and often on a part-time basis. It was from those days that the term municipal clerk had its origins. To the degree that administrative or political challenges arose, with the possible exception of the larger urban municipalities, these were most often dealt with by the mayor and members of council with little or no involvement of the municipal clerk. This was the historical antecedent of the council-committee system.

As noted in Chapter I, change in the type and volume of responsibilities expected of municipalities came slowly in the years leading up to WWII. But as the expectations of local government grew in the second half of this century, change has been coming in a torrent. The result of the massive change in the role of the municipal institution has meant that elected councillors could no longer be reasonably expected to act as administrators as well as policy makers. With the old system, overworked and underpaid councillors did much of the administrative and clerical work, but it ceased to be a practical answer for the needs and problems facing larger towns and cities of the region.

Something was needed to provide for greater policy and administrative co-ordination. The answer was sought in the American *City Manager* system. While the United States motivation for this innovation involved stripping local councils of their power to engage in political corruption, the Canadian approach was to adapt the managerial system to the cause of more effective administration. Council needed to be relieved from the day-to-day running of the municipality and to be supported, more fully, in their role as policy makers. In the Canadian version the manager made council more effective without diminishing its power.

In the Maritime provinces, the senior official in a council-manager system may often have a title other than "manager". The most common alternative title is "Chief Administrative Officer (CAO)", although words such as "administrator" or "clerk" are also used. What is important in characterizing the system is not a matter of titles, but rather the organizational and functional relationship between municipal staff and council. In some municipal units, organizational charts may be just as misleading as any title. More than once the authors have undertaken consulting projects on behalf of municipalities which supposedly have adopted council-manager systems, but which in practice continue to operate on a committee system.

The council-manager system is based upon a premise of separation between policy and administration. Council is to be responsible for making policy, while staff through the manager is responsible for administration. This task separation is intended to free the council from routine administrative matters, allowing it to concentrate on its policy making role. The manager is expected see that council decisions are carried out, and at the same time to co-ordinate the various branches of the administration. The typical administrative duties would include hiring practices, supervision of department heads, overseeing the preparation of annual estimates for council's budget deliberations, administering and enforcing municipal by-laws, preparing and presenting reports to council and generally keeping the council appraised of matters of importance to the community.

This system vests a large amount of responsibility in the hands of the manager, which may become a source of frustration to any council that would prefer to have a more hands-on approach. This can be particularly problematic for new councillors who are either unclear or unsure of their policy making role or who had expected a job that would wield administrative clout.

Committees do exist in the council-manager system, but their function is primarily to examine policy alternatives, to seek the views of the public and to provide advice to council. They have no direct role in the supervision or management of any municipal department or service.

The Process

The two previous sections of this chapter have described the framework and structures of local government and have identified the principal participants. This was a static snapshot of the municipal decision-making apparatus. In this final section of the chapter, we turn to a more dynamic perspective of how systems operate in practice.

Government Versus Governing

When we think of "government" we often visualize the structures that house our governments and the individuals who operate them. At the Federal level, we might include the House of Commons, the Senate, the Cabinet, the Prime Minister's Office, the Privy Council Office, and the bureaucracy. Similar structures would come to mind at the provincial levels. For the municipal level we think primarily of the municipal offices, the council and the administrative staff. A description of these structures, while useful, does not convey any real appreciation for the process of governing.

We may broaden our thinking by considering some of the processes and activities which take place within these structural frameworks, such as election campaigns, the throne speech, the budget speech, legislative debate and scrutiny, the notorious question period, the development of policies and delivery of programs. At the municipal level somewhat comparable processes exist, although some of the local governmental activities are less formal or less well defined. But whatever the level, while combining structures with activities may give us further insight into government, it still seems to fall short of describing what is involved in *governing.*

To discover the essence of governing, let us to look at the whole picture in a more abstract way. Municipalities are made up of individuals and groups with various needs, beliefs, interests, and aspirations. Their differences all have an impact on demands placed upon public policy. For example, one group of citizens may highly value the natural environment and demand its protection, while other groups may place greater emphasis on economic development and financial prosperity. Thus, what is important to one person or group may be unimportant or possibly even threatening to others.

Let us examine a hypothetical situation. Let us assume there is a large wooded area, owned by the municipality, which your council wants to develop. One group of citizens wants to see a municipal park created in order to gain more recreational opportunities for young people who now hang out at the local mall. Another group, while sympathetic to the park idea, prefer the possibility of improving the tax base and feel that a combination of residential and commercial development would be the best use of the land. Some compromise, ultimately, may be possible, but clearly satisfying the interests of one group will be at the expense of the other. How then will two different and conflicting sets of interests be resolved? The answer to this question is to describe the process of governing.

A political body, be it a parliament, a legislature or a municipal council is where a society's conflicting interests are presented for deliberation and resolution. Such resolution through a political process is the essence of governing. In a democracy this process must be successful more often than not, but more importantly it must generally be seen to be working. History teaches that when people lose faith that the governing process is fair, they will be tempted to look for less constructive ways of asserting their interests.

Governing and Conflict Resolution

The model is a useful illustration of the process of conflict resolution. Several assumptions underlie this process, the first being that the role of the political entity, the municipal council, is simply to listen and deliberate. The second assumes that all individuals or groups are equally competent to affect outcomes, but as we all know, for a variety of reasons this is not often the case. In pursuing their interests or "rights", some individuals and groups have considerable resources such as access to information or professional staff and have no problems in advancing their interests. On the other hand, others lack either skills and/or resources to do the same thing. This imbalance, if left unchecked, could significantly

Governing of Conflict Resolution

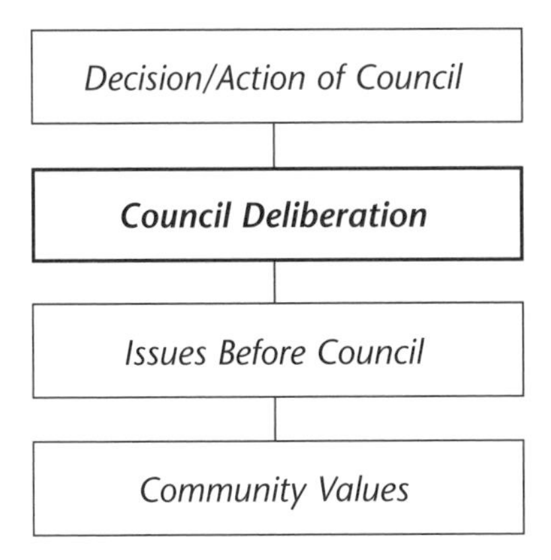

skew public policy. The elected official therefore must be alert to all points of view when considering matters of public policy.

Dual Roles of Municipal Government

As we have previously discussed, municipal government performs two distinct roles: a political or governing role; and its administrative or service delivery role.

The basis for the political role of local government lies in its ability to identify and respond to a diversity of needs of its citizens. Because of limited resources and competing interests, choices have to be made, and in the making of these choices lies local government's political role. The range of choices will undoubtedly continue to change over time, as will public expectations of what kinds of issues should be of concern to local governments. At one time they had significant authority over services now provided at the provincial level. We need only think of matters such as health, education and welfare, all of which have passed beyond both control and influence of the local level. New challenges have appeared as municipal governments have assumed active roles in matters of planning, recreation, economic development and environmental protection issues. Each of these involve political choices and all have potential for competitive conflicts.

The other, more traditional, role of municipal government is in service delivery. Here the role is to deliver services over which it has varying degrees of discretion. In some instances, the municipality acts as a conduit providing services whose nature and standards have been determined at a senior level of government. Examples include policing, garbage collection and landfill, sewage disposal, and collection of provincial property tax levies for education and other purposes. Other municipal services, while not closely regulated by the province, have a degree of inflexibility in their levels and costs. Street and sidewalk maintenance, water utilities, fire protection, street lighting, and maintenance of administrative and public works buildings, are examples of service budgetary items that remain fairly predictable from one year to the next.

In summary, there is a political role consistent with the notion of municipal government as a governing body. In service delivery the role involves a more passive responsibility that is essentially administrative.

Relationships

Council-Staff

The relationship between council and staff is an important element in the daily life of every municipal government. When the rapport between the two sides is based on mutual respect and a sense of shared purpose, the task of governing will be greatly furthered. Conversely, when elements of hostility, discontent, or suspicion creep into the relationship, the lines of communication will wither and the decision making process will grind to a halt.

As was noted earlier, there is a basic division of responsibility that signifies that council has responsibility for policy and staff for administration. This distinction between policy and administration, however, is usually neither clear nor sharp and in real life often involves considerable ambiguity or uncertainty. A common situation arises when inexperienced councillors feel that they have a right to intervene in administrative problems, while in the face of council inertia, department heads assume the right to make policy decisions. What may initially start out as a routine administrative matter could quickly blossom into a political ruckus. It is in situations like these that the relationship between council and staff can become acrimonious.

The experience of the senior administrative officer and of council will be important in coming to a mutual understanding of what is the work of staff and what is the work of council. The relationship between the roles of staff and council may vary from one unit to another, depending on the type and size of the unit and its organizational structure. Nevertheless, there are common principles that ought to be recognized in all municipal units. First, in order to provide quality advice to council, the administration as a whole needs to understand and value the political role of council. Second, council needs to understand and value the administrative role of staff in order to place realistic demands upon all of its members, and third, council and staff need to maintain both formal and informal channels of communication and act quickly to resolve potential conflicts.

Accountability

To Citizens

A municipality may be seen as a public organization that exists in order to meet the range of needs of a community and its citizens. From this perspective, local government could be considered an instrument of the collective will of all residents within its boundaries. For better or worse, however, the Canadian constitution makes the relationship between citizens and their municipal units subject to legislation and directives of their provincial governments. Thus the local council has basic accountability to its provincial authority, usually through the government minister responsible for municipal affairs. In effect the provincial level has veto power with respect to a range of council decisions, a power that emphasizes the upward accountability obligation. On the other hand, accountability to the electorate of the municipality is more tenuous: it is only during elections that individual members of council can be rewarded or punished for their part in decisions made during their terms of office.

Council-Staff

The principle of accountability should be firmly defined in the relationship between council and the municipal staff. In a council-committee system, service heads have a reporting relationship to council through particular committees that oversee their departments. In the municipal manager system, the department heads report to the manager or CAO, who, in turn, is the only staff member directly accountable to council. In either system, however, it is important to ensure that in matters of personnel administration, council's role should not go beyond the establishment of policies. Application of such policies should, in both cases, be the responsibility of the administrative head of the municipality. When council as a whole or any of its members involve themselves in matters affecting individual employees, the authority of the manager or clerk is obviously undermined. An administration with this type of situation is obviously in trouble!

Municipality - Province

In previous publications, the authors have argued that the power of provinces over their municipalities may be absolute in constitutional law, but that in practice, local government derives its most important power from its ability to mobilize its citizens against unreasonable provincial policy decisions.[4] In recent years, for example, we have witnessed the successful resistance of New Brunswick communities to provincial pressure for forced amalgamations, such as happened in the cases of the Saint John urban area; the proposed union of Moncton, Dieppe, and Riverview; and Campbellton-Atholville. On the other hand, we have also seen dramatic examples of municipal amalgamation decrees imposed by Ontario and Nova Scotia in the face of vigorous opposition from affected citizens and councils. We must accordingly to some degree modify our previous views on the ability of citizens to always shield their local governments from arbitrary exercise of provincial power.

The Issue of Party Politics

Political parties as such are not part of the municipal landscape in the Maritime provinces. Party organization and policy platforms are, officially, absent from municipal elections. Candidates run for office on the basis of their individual policy platforms and are elected as independent candidates. This stands in rather sharp contrast to the highly organized party machinery that is such a prominent feature of provincial and federal elections.

Most municipal officials in the Maritimes embrace the idea that the absence of political parties is desirable and worth preserving. This view is predicated on the somewhat ambiguous notion that local government is somehow more virtuous without the involvement of party politics.

A more balanced view is that the introduction of a party system at the local level would offer both opportunities and perils. Advantages would be most apparent at election time, since the electorate would have the opportunity to vote on the basis of clear policy alternatives. Once a municipal party has gained power, the electorate can hold both the party and its candidates accountable for promises made at election time. Moreover there would be an opposition party to remind the governing party of its public commitments and responsibilities. Whenever these are not discharged appropriately, the opposition would be ready to alert the public to the shortcomings of the governing party.

4 See for example, *Guide to Local Government in Nova Scotia, Third Edition.* Halifax: Henson College, 1992, pages 23-24.

The relatively weak executive function at the local government level would be significantly strengthened with the introduction of a party system. Local and even parochial issues tend to dominate discussions in council sessions. This makes it difficult to develop a broader and more comprehensive vision for the municipality. Far too often, municipalities never rise above reacting to events that have already happened. This constant focus on the past does not help in the process of planning for the future!

The major objection to a municipal party system is that it would narrow access to the political process. The selection of candidates, the greater cost of political campaigns, and the higher profile of partisan candidates may all combine to discourage citizens from offering for office. Indeed it may be that the absence of highly "professionalized" standards at the municipal level has been a key factor in attracting individuals to seek council office. In the absence of party involvement, most candidates for office see their engagement as an extension of their commitment to the community.

Any initiative towards introduction of a party system at the local level would run into strongly held sentiments in favour of the *status quo*. The rough and tumble of provincial and federal politics has done little to raise the image of the party system in the minds of the public and has tended to reinforce resistance to overt party involvement in municipal affairs. On the other hand, the public is generally fully aware of the party affiliations of their individual council members, which offers an interesting study in political correctness!

Summary

As the third level of government, municipalities have been described as being the level closest to the people, but at the same time as being creatures of the provinces. In consequence, the study of local government must of necessity focus a good deal of attention on how it responds to its two masters. On the one hand, the electorate increasingly expects not only efficiency in the delivery of municipal services at affordable tax rates, but also looks to its council members to protect the environment, to create or maintain a business climate that will maximize employment, and to chart a futures plan that will enhance quality of life in the community. On the other hand, the municipality must respond to rules and policies handed down from its provincial superiors. Between these two sometimes opposing pressures, the tasks of local government revolve around a mixture of routine administration, crisis management, and meeting challenges of probable change.

In this chapter we have reviewed the structures and the participants in this undertaking. We have examined the processes that are involved in making the decisions that go into its administration and governance. The issue of accountability has been discussed, as well as that of political parties and their supposed absence from municipal politics.

Chapter VI

Public Participation[1]

Citizens no longer see public participation as an "opportunity", graciously granted by the council and administration; it is regarded as a basic service and an integral part of local governance.[2]

What is Public Participation?

Increasingly, individuals and citizen groups are demanding more direct involvement in local government decision making. A practical problem often occurs when municipal councils fail to offer a positive response to such demands. Instead of trying to understand the value of public participation, they may engage in a futile debate on its desirability.

Public participation may be defined as the *continued active involvement* of *citizens in making the policies which affect them.* To some degree, public participation always exists where there is a democracy, but during the past few decades, the appearance of organized citizen groups in response to a variety of issues has given emphasis to the idea. Local government has often been seen as being unduly influenced by the development industry or by other business lobbyists. Citizens seeking a voice are frequently reacting to proposals that they consider contrary to a broader public interest.

The public has a right to expect that both elected and administrative officials recognize participation as a legitimate means of ensuring that proposed changes do not benefit one class of citizens at the expense of another. Properly understood, it can help to avoid the polarization of relations that sometimes threatens the effectiveness of municipal government and is disruptive to the democratic process.

1 Some parts of this chapter are based on text prepared by Professor James McNiven for the first edition of *A Guide to Local Government in Nova Scotia*, published by the Institute of Public Affairs, Dalhousie University, 1977.
2 Catherine A. Graham and Susan D. Phillips (eds.) *Citizen Engagement: Lessons in Participation from Local Government.* Toronto: Institute of Public Administration of Canada, 1998, p.2.

Issues for Public Concern

In the Maritime provinces, issues that arouse public sensitivity are often centred on planning and land use decisions. Proposals for landfill and recycling locations, sewage treatment plants, housing developments, commercial rezoning, industrial parks, recreation facilities, and disposal of former park, playground or other public lands, are the kinds of topics that are likely to capture public attention. They include policy matters that directly affect the quality of life in any community, so citizens have a substantial stake in decisions and need to be prepared for vigorous participation in the process. For elected officials, attempting to handle such subjects without adequate citizen consultation is a recipe for discord and distrust.

Who Participates?

Not everyone gets involved in public participation activities. The cliche that "if we let everybody participate, society would become an anarchy" is just so much nonsense, because only a small proportion of the total population is prepared to expend the time and effort that public participation requires. Depending upon the nature of the issue at hand, somewhere between one-half of one percent (0.5%) and twenty percent (20%) of a given population will do the minimum necessary to be called participants. If there is a crisis, such as a strike or a demonstration, the higher percentage could be reached. Day-to-day participation is likely to involve very modest numbers.

There is cause for concern if it is left to only a small number of citizens to express their interest in what happens in their local government. These would often represent the more affluent members of society who are best able to pursue their personal biases and to order things as they would like to see them. To counter-balance this influence, it is a healthy sign when a broader spectrum of citizens make the effort to become involved in public participation organizations. They may be young students, ambitious farmers, labour union members, housewives or senior citizens. What they have in common is the will to mobilize others who share their views. They may lack money to exercise influence quietly, but they can make their presence felt by making use of reliable information, and being assertive in demanding that their voices be heard.

Who participates? The answer depends on the determination of all citizens to preserve local government as a vital instrument for local democracy. Since many people find themselves individually unable to affect policy, they need to seek out friends and neighbours who have the necessary energy and skills to provide organizational leadership.

How to Make Your Voices Heard

An individual may seem a lonely figure in the arena of public policy. But when someone feels strongly about community issues, or is offended by some abuse to the environment, or feels outraged when justice appears to be blind, that person obviously needs to speak out. In Canada, setting up a soap box in a public park is not a very effective way of changing decisions about public policies. In any case, single issues may not be the main purpose of wanting to speak out. It may involve frustration about the general direction or running of your local government. So it is useful to examine what alternatives are available.

Electoral Participation

Democracy implies the right of citizens to participate in the process of government. The most familiar type of participation is in the electoral system where citizens have the opportunity to vote for the persons responsible for formulating and adopting public policies. At the provincial and federal level, the party system assists voters in identifying how individual candidates will exercise these responsibilities, and people who are anxious to participate more directly in policy matters can do so by joining a political party.

As we have discussed in Chapter V, the party system is not a feature of the way local government operates In the Maritime provinces. Civic voters cannot readily identify how effectively a particular candidate will represent their interests, since councils are made up of individuals without commitment to any set of common policies. Council members are elected for fixed terms of three years, so there is no way of changing legislators between elections. Unlike the provincial or federal levels, there is no "vote of confidence" process that can bring down an unpopular administration.

Before municipal government became involved with matters such as environmental protection, social services, recreation, and the whole area of community planning, political decisions were largely confined to administrative matters. Elected representatives were primarily "watchdogs"; they were charged with responsibility for seeing that routine services were efficiently performed, that proper accounting was kept of public expenditures, and that the tax rate was kept down.

In Chapter I we explored how, in the years following World War II, the range of services that people expected from their local governments increased dramatically. Thus decisions in council chambers became of much broader public interest, and citizens began to search for effective means of expressing their needs and wants. Public housing, downtown preservation, economic development, solid waste management, shopping malls, public transit, heritage preservation, fairness of property and other taxes, zoning and development proposals, municipal amalgamation, and intergovernmental relations are among the main topics of public debate in modern society. The electoral process is obviously not adequate, by itself, to translate community concerns on these issues into action.

Lobbying

Lobbying, a word that carries a not wholly deserved flavour, is probably the most widespread form of public input into governmental processes the world over. Both individuals and organizations need to deal with their governments, and governments at different levels need to communicate with each other, to make their interests and concerns known. There is nothing improper in approaching legislators at all three levels to express particular viewpoints. Indeed, organizations that speak for various interest groups, such as Boards of Trade, professional organizations, labour unions, or residents' associations, are important and necessary to keep elected officials aware of what is happening in the broader community. Lobbying is only improper where there is an offer of material gain to the elected official in order to influence his or her vote.

To be effective, both individuals and community organizations need to understand and become skilfull in lobby techniques. Methods commonly used include mass letters and petitions, letters to the editor, individual and group approaches to elected officials, and more assertive measures such as demonstrations, boycotts, and sit-ins. In major confrontations on single issues, interest groups are likely to form coalitions with others who may share a common concern on the issue being addressed.

Getting on Council Agenda

As a citizen, how do you get your voice heard at a municipal council meeting? To many people, addressing their council is a matter of right. In reality, however, no citizen has any more right to be heard at a council meeting than he or she would have to appear before the provincial legislature or federal parliament. As summarized in an official information flyer issued by one of the Maritime provinces, the matter is as follows:

> It is a basic rule of parliamentary procedure (so basic that it is unwritten) that no one has the power to address Council without permission. This is also true of Parliament and the House of Assembly. The meeting is a meeting of Council not of the public. Council has the power to choose who can speak. No one has the right to do so.

A citizen who wishes to address council therefore must request an invitation. At certain times when planning decisions are being considered, there may be an open invitation to members of the public to speak on particular issues. Otherwise, an approach to the office of the mayor, to a council member or to the municipal clerk may provide the desired invitation.

In the case of villages in Nova Scotia and in New Brunswick, and communities in Prince Edward Island, respective laws provide that annual public meetings must be held for the purpose of passing the budget. At these meetings, members of the public are entitled to attend as participants.

Special Purpose Bodies

Public participation activities are not limited to those involving council or its individual members. There are a number of other points where citizens have opportunities to participate or influence decision making. It should be recalled that local government administers some of its services through a number of boards and commissions originally set up to distance them from possible political interference. Such bodies have also been seen as a way of involving a broader range of citizens in the business of government. In this way, the community may benefit from a broad range of expertise in overseeing the management of public services. As the complexity of many services and local government functions have increased, an added argument for this dispersal of authority has been the need for expert and professional advice on a broad range of subjects. From these combined pressures have come the present proliferation of special purpose, semi-autonomous bodies, such as utilities commissions, social service committees, regional development commissions, district school boards, library boards, police commissions, and numerous others.

Distinct from boards and commissions that have acquired substantial management independence are bodies established to provide advice and to serve as a link between citizens and council. Such committees are able to secure input from citizen groups and from professionals in the community without infringing on the basic decision-making responsibilities of council. Primary examples of this type of body are the planning advisory committees established under provincial planning legislation.

Advisory committees have often proven to be an effective means for citizens to make their views known early in the planning process. Through public hearings, intensive study, and in formulating new ideas and recommendations to council, the committee can be an important avenue for citizens to make their views known as well as to secure access to information in a direct and timely manner.

Special Purpose Participation

So far, we have considered those means of participation that are directed towards influence on council decisions. We now turn to the kinds of public involvement that most often arise in single issue situations. A proposal to locate a municipal incinerator or land-fill site in a particular location, or a plan for redevelopment of buildings with heritage significance, or the re-zoning of residential lands for industrial purposes, are examples of issues that have given rise to the formation of neighbourhood or citizen action committees. These kinds of movements have illustrated the power of people, when aroused, to influence policy very directly. Some members of council view this type of participation negatively, while others recognize the rights of citizens to choose whatever means are available within the law to express and defend their interests.

Citizens' groups, whether formed to fight for single issues or more broadly-based to voice community or neighbourhood concerns, can be a valuable means of ensuring that council remains accountable to the electorate. Citizens need to insist that municipal staff provide easy access to information, that public hearings are held on important issues, and that council members undertake to attend meetings of citizen groups whenever the opportunity arises.

Participation from the Elected Councillor's Viewpoint

For an elected official who is interested in both serving the public effectively and in continuing to do so, some facts must be kept in mind concerning public participation.

First, those involved are part of the public. While an elected official may represent "the people", it must be remembered that in the Canadian system, especially at the municipal level, only a minority of people, and often only a minority of voters, actually approved his or her candidacy. The "people" are a diverse lot of individuals whose interests can fluctuate greatly between elections. Those who did not care enough to vote in the last election may be aroused by an issue that poses a threat to their welfare or peace of mind. Regardless of legalisms, some of these citizens are unlikely to wait patiently for the next election campaign.

Secondly, those who become involved in public participation organizations are also those likely to lend their skills and talents to future election campaigns. Their goodwill could be important in winning re-election.

Thirdly, if one looks at the political process as one of problem solving, citizen groups can be of positive assistance to the elected official. Such groups may act as an early warning device, informing councils of potential and real problems in the community; rarely do groups function without some degree of wider popular support and concern. Citizen groups may also be useful in providing solutions to problems. Normally, these groups spring up because their members feel more threatened by a situation than do other people (granted there are also a number of busybodies who get involved in everything, but it is unwise to label all participants as such). People who are involved are more likely to have given a lot of thought to the problem, and their views may carry the seeds of an equitable and useful solution.

Taking Advantage of Participation

Public participation has been criticized not because it leads to bad decisions on the part of a council or the local administration; it rarely does. Participation does, however, complicate the process of arriving at decisions. Normally the decisions are better, but they may take longer to make than would otherwise be the case.

The situation is due partly to the fact that when participation is encouraged, more people want to become involved. More important even than numbers is the degree of expertise in participation possessed by those who become active. Research has pointed out that it is easier to organize people against something than it is to get them to support an idea. Compare how hard it is to enlist people in a community betterment campaign or in supporting the United Way, to the ease of organizing groups to stop some road project or prevent demolition of an historic building. The "negative" project will gain vocal supporters more easily. A crisis can be provoked which will draw far more interest and activity than any "positive" project can generate. Since positive participation is much harder to develop than negative participation, most local pressure groups start their existence by being against something. The challenge to participants is to move to the stage of promoting positive ideas as well.

Positive participation can only result if local officials and administrators agree to work with local citizen groups wherever possible. The question facing local governments is whether to hold them to a "negative" stage, fighting continual battles, or to accept and include them in the design of a community satisfactory to everybody. This latter approach takes time and effort on the part of both sides, especially at first—and it means some honest sharing of responsibility. As citizens gain expertise in making their interests known, however, the process should become more efficient. Unfortunately, there is no easy, magic solution. Citizens need to recognize that council members and staff are often tempted to simply "get on with the job". Only by working towards a relationship of mutual respect will the interests of the whole community be adequately served.

Consultation

The key to productive participation is consultation. There are at least four degrees of consultation that both parties should seek to cultivate:

1. The most basic is the communication of issues to the public. Often municipal officials look on this as a waste, especially where it requires the spending of money on advertising. But it must be remembered that communication helps to sort out issues on the basis of importance. Most problems may be of little interest to most people, but the real crises occurs when the elected officials, rather than the people themselves, try to judge this importance and make mistakes. Open and positive communication may cause political noise, but secret decisions that become public can unnecessarily generate messy situations and a good deal of mistrust.

2. The next most important form of consultation is the gathering of advice. Good political and community advisors can help any official steer a calm and productive path. This is especially important in avoiding the wrong decision, as opposed to making the right one. There is a difference, if you think about it. Even doing nothing about a problem can be classed as a decision.

3. The third level of consultation is the most noted form of participation. That is the meeting of public officials with community groups to clarify concerns and interests with regard to particular issues. This may take place in a confrontation mode, which is painful to endure. It may take place in formal hearings, which are time-consuming. It may come as a result of trying to gain information for decision making. It is impossible to always be co-operative, attentive and deferential, but it is wise for both officials and the public to not move into situations which can be disastrous in outcome. The more important a decision is, the more likely it is that both elected officials and citizens will have strong opinions. The mixture of these influences on the decision must reflect the mixture of such strong opinions if there is to be a workable solution.

4. Finally, there will always be issues where opinion in the community is very strong and very pervasive. "Everybody" is agitated. These important issues should be decided by the community. A wise council will pass them back, perhaps in plebiscites or general meetings. There is a time for a representative to make a decision for a community but there also may come a time when the mental health and moral fibre of a community require that the representative step aside in favour of overall participation.

It is a judgement call to decide on what issues, when, and how these varying degrees of consultation may be employed. Most of the knack of sensing the status of an issue is made up of common sense. At a minimum, however, there should be good publicity on all issues. This is important for both the local government officials and for the leadership of community organizations. It is a useful "insurance policy" for both parties against nasty surprises.

Summary

People need to become politically involved with their local government as long as there is change going on about them—representative government or not. Normally, continuous involvement may be restricted to elected politicians and a small segment of citizens who are especially sensitive to local issues. Likewise, more people may become involved if change is needed, but does not appear to be taking place. Since this involvement is inevitable, unthinking resistance to it by elected officials will generally be politically unproductive.

A more sensible alternative is to strive for an ongoing process of information exchange between citizens and their elected representatives. This takes patience and trust, because normally councillors want to press on with their tasks, while citizen groups must strive to go beyond "negative" participation to "positive" participation. This can only occur when consultation is ongoing between the elected officials and the active citizens.

Consultation may be at four levels of intensity as previously described. Minimally, citizens should be informed of all issues requiring decisions, so that they have an opportunity to express their interests. On those issues of little importance, elected officials should seek advice from community leaders and those organizing pressure groups. More important issues require a process of formal hearings, possible confrontations, and fact-finding inquiries. Where the issue is of community-wide importance, the elected official may be in the difficult position of having to reconcile personal views and the public mood with the legal obligation imposed on council by provincial planning legislation.

Chapter VII

Municipal Finance

"The art of taxation consists in so plucking the goose as to obtain the largest amount of feathers with the least amount of hissing." Colbert

Introduction

Municipal revenue sources in the Maritimes, in common with elsewhere in Canada, most often appear to be insufficient to finance ever increasing costs of local services. This cost increase is related not only to a greater range of services needed as a result of urban growth, but the substance of services is also becoming more sophisticated as new social and environmental needs are identified. Such costs invariably outstrips any natural growth in available revenues. The resulting shortfall is commonly referred to as the fiscal gap. Bridging this gap, without unacceptable hardship for citizenry, is a familiar topic on the agendas of all municipal councils.

To cope with this recurring challenge requires a search for innovative approaches by both council and staff. Unfortunately, a common reaction is to focus on expenditure cuts in a way that creates more problems than it solves. Under pressures of the moment, possible alternatives seem too complex or too remote. Measures such as joint action with neighbouring municipalities, private-public sector partnerships, enlisting ideas from community groups or working with the volunteer community, or even considering amalgamation with other units, may all be dismissed as requiring too much effort and involving too much change. Without such a broader vision, however, councillors may be shortchanging their real leadership responsibilities.

It is, of course, useful to recall that local governments have limited powers to innovate. As noted repeatedly in this book, municipal units are "creatures" of their provincial governments. This subservience holds true in a variety of fields, and that of municipal finance is no exception. The provinces, for example, have consistently denied municipalities access to more lucrative and flexible sources of revenue such as sales or income tax. Indeed, municipalities must dutifully manage their financial affairs within narrow limits imposed by provincial legislation and regulation.

The financial health of municipal units became of serious concern to provincial governments during the Great Depression of the 1930's. With the collapse of the overheated economy of the 1920's, markets plunged and industries closed, throwing millions of people out of work in the developed countries of the world. In Canada, a series of droughts in western provinces played havoc with the national agricultural economy, adding to unemployment distress in the towns and cities of the whole country. Without protection of the social safety net familiar to present generations, both rural and urban residents were rendered helpless in huge numbers. As a result, many local governments faced insolvency as tax revenues plummeted while bankruptcy wiped out businesses large and small and poor relief costs soared.

From that point onwards, provincial governments were forced to take measures to ensure that municipalities lived within their financial means and that their capital debt was carefully controlled. This concern has continued to the present day. It is clear that the recent wave of forced amalgamation of municipalities in each of the Maritime provinces has been brought about partly by concern for the financial viability of affected municipal units. But this persistent provincial fear that, left to their own devices, municipalities will likely wind up with financial problems, almost becomes a self-fulfilling prophecy. Under pressure to be efficient and innovative, yet at the same time lacking both resources and necessary independence to allow for experimentation, local governments are prone to blunder into financial dead-ends. In this reality lies the principal municipal conundrum.

The following sections will examine the relationship between revenue sources and service demands, and will explore the search for balance in the equation.

Revenues

Property tax levied on real property located within the municipal boundaries is the principal component of "own source revenues". This is the one taxation source over which municipalities have some degree of independent control and is the revenue field most closely identified with the municipal level. Other non-tax revenue include user fees,[1] licences and

1 In New Brunswick there is no clear legal authority on which municipalities can charge user fees, except when a separate utility has been established for water and sewer services.

permits, rentals of municipal property or equipment, sale of services, and fines for infractions of municipal by-laws. These types of revenue are usually of lesser significance and are generally more directly related to specific services.

Property Tax

The property tax is essentially a tax on wealth, as contrasted with income tax, which is based on earnings. A person may have a substantial home with a large area in an exclusive neighbourhood, but may, for a variety of reasons, have little or no income. Even if the person is "wealthy" in terms of property, the assessed value does not address the question of the owner's ability to pay a tax levy that requires a substantial annual cash outlay.

This limitation is perhaps a principal reason why provincial and federal governments have long since ceased to rely on property-based taxes as their main source of revenues. Accordingly, this form of taxation has been left mainly to local levels of government. Since municipalities are considered to need a smaller bite of the total revenue pie, their taxation is felt to be modest enough so that their levies will cause little real hardship.

The property tax is, therefore, the one significant tax source available to municipal governments in the Maritime provinces. It is relatively easy to administer, particularly in New Brunswick and Prince Edward Island where the provinces act as collection agencies both for their own property tax levies as well as for those of their municipal units. The tax is reasonably straight-forward and simple to calculate, compared to other taxes such as income tax. Collection is not difficult, since the tax remains a lien on property until paid, which means that the provincial or municipal authority issuing the tax bills has the power to order sale of properties when payment arrears are outstanding. Finally, property tax is generally, if reluctantly, accepted by the community as one of life's inevitable realities!

On the other hand, many municipal officials, elected and appointed, have serious criticisms of the property tax and the way it is applied. First, by itself it is not considered adequate to meet the revenue needs of many municipal governments. The tax is not buoyant, that is, it does not respond well to changes in economic conditions. When the economy is performing well there is no corresponding increase in tax yield from the property tax. On the other hand, municipal councillors are often highly sensitive to impacts of any increase on their constituents, and therefore are reluctant to accept upward adjustments. This may also be due to the property tax's high visibility, which ensures that changes will quickly be noted. A comparable change in income tax might hardly be noticed by the vast majority of taxpayers who have that tax deducted at source.

A second and major objection is the regressive nature of the tax. Thus, individuals at the lower end of the income scale pay a higher percentage of their income on property tax than those at the higher end. The tax is clearly regressive because regardless of income, one must purchase a minimum level of shelter, often in the form of rent. Landlords naturally strive to pass on property tax increases to their tenants. In recognition of this impact on low income households, many municipalities have introduced programs which provide various forms of tax forgiveness or relief. At any rate, as long as the range of services to be financed from the tax remains relatively narrow, the impact on individuals is sufficiently tolerable so that the inequities do not loom large enough to cause major protest.

Administration of Property Taxation in the Maritimes

As noted, this tax is based on a levy on the assessed value of land and buildings. The amount of an individual tax bill is calculated by multiplying the assessed value of each property by the tax rate. Municipal tax rates are set by councils as part of their annual budget process, and there are usually different rates for different classes of property such as residential, commercial, farm or forest property. In New Brunswick and Prince Edward Island, each province bills and collects the tax on behalf of its municipalities, together with a provincial property tax levy. How tax rates are set will be dealt with more fully under the section dealing with budgeting.

A variant of the municipal property tax in Nova Scotia and Prince Edward Island is the area rate. This is used primarily to recover costs of services specific to a particular locale within a municipality, such as a particular subdivision, fire district, village or a service commission. It may be levied on the assessed value of real property to finance specific services such as street lighting, fire protection, recreation, and garbage collection, but it may also be charged on frontage or on a per property basis. In county or rural district municipalities where sewer piping may serve pockets of population density, the area rate may be specific to properties served by hookups.

Area rates, as such, are not used in New Brunswick, but where there are differing levels of service in a municipality, council may decide to levy differing tax rates within its boundaries.

Some writers consider the property tax an appropriate form of taxation for services to property, as opposed to services to people. This view is based upon an assumption that services such as sewer, water, curbs and sidewalks increase the value of property and accordingly, owners should bear their cost. Others dismiss this distinction between services to people and services to property as being artificial, since all services ultimately are for people. Those who hold the first view use it as a basis for the division of responsibility between municipal and provincial government, arguing that since the provincial governments in all three provinces have complete control of services such as education, social services and justice, these people services should not rely on any form of municipal support.

In its 1995-96 program of service exchange, Nova Scotia accepted the property/people distinction. While it has taken on administrative responsibility, however, the province is still forcing municipal units to include a provincial education levy in their tax bills and to contribute to social and correctional services which now are totally provincial responsibilities.

A Primer on Assessment

Assessment is the process of establishing a specific dollar value of real property, i.e., buildings and land, for purposes of taxation. Before the massive 1967 program of Equal Opportunities in New Brunswick, assessment was undertaken by individual municipalities, but was subsequently assumed by the province. Prince Edward Island followed suit shortly after, and, in 1977, Nova Scotia became the last of the Maritime provinces to accept this task.

The rationale for these provincial take-overs was based on the principle that assessment ought to be a neutral and essentially technical service which should be beyond political control of any council. As a provincial function, it is work that is best performed by a specialized, highly trained, staff of assessors working with a standard set of province-wide procedures.

Assessment must be concerned with the notion of equity or fairness. Essentially this means that properties of similar class and value should have similar assessments, and conversely, properties of substantially different characteristics should have dissimilar assessments. For example, if in a community a particular property is assessed at an $80,000.00 market value, similar properties in comparable locations within the community should be assessed at the same value. Both owners should therefore be subject to the same property tax. On the other hand, if your neighbour's house is larger and more luxurious and is assessed to have a market value twice as large as yours, his or her assessed value should be double that of yours with the owner paying twice as much property tax. From an equity perspective, the actual assessed value assigned to your house is less important than that relative relationships between properties.

In the three Maritime provinces, courts have interpreted legislation to mean that *fair market value* should be the basis for assessment. This value is defined as what a willing buyer would pay to a willing seller for a particular property, with neither party under duress. To arrive at an estimate of likely values for individual properties under these conditions, assessors first analyze information on recent real estate transactions in any particular area. Such sales data are combined with information on location features, the size and style of property, value of improvements, construction materials, replacement cost, and in the case of revenue producing properties, gross income. All such factors are taken into account, but in final property valuations, some measure of subjective judgement must be made by the property assessor.

The real estate market is a moving target. When prices are rising, there should be corresponding increases in the general level of assessment. If reassessments are made on a yearly basis, such increases are usually mild enough to cause only moderate grumbling. But grumbling turns to torrents of outrage when reassessments are made only at intervals of three or more years[2] and percentage increases in market value reach into double digit numbers. Property owners demand explanations for increases in assessed value without corresponding physical improvements having been made to properties. The link between a particular assessment value and increases in general real estate market values is often difficult to grasp, as is the idea that an assessment increase does not mean an automatic increase in an owner's tax bill.

Critics of property tax point out the distortions that often creep in. One is the tendency to over-assess new buildings in comparison to older ones. Then there is the sheer magnitude of the task of assessing huge numbers of properties, which makes it physically impossible for assessors to follow market value fluctuations resulting from change in use, economic conditions, neighbourhood environment, or other factors. Such distortions are magnified when fiscal restraint causes reductions in the number of assessors, cuts the size of training budgets, and further postpones the day when credible reassessments can be made on a yearly basis.

2 In New Brunswick, there is a five-year cycle for property value reassessments.

Assessment Appeal Process

An owner who feels that an assessment is unjust or in error has the right to appeal. In each province the appeal process is designed to offer a simple procedure with a minimum of formality or need for legal counsel. Common grounds for such appeals includes errors in the description of property such as its dimensions or physical condition, or lack of consistency in the estimation of value as compared to other properties elsewhere in the community.

The notice of assessment will generally contain the information needed to initiate an appeal, including the deadline for its filing. An appeal usually starts out as a purely administrative process in the regional assessment office. If unresolved at this level, the appeal can be taken to the assessment appeal tribunal or court. Here proceedings are conducted very informally. Normally the only persons present at such hearings are the chairman of the court; the assessor who carried out the assessment; and the person making the appeal. The chair's decision is often announced at the end of the hearing. Should the appellant claim an error in law in the decision, there is a right to appeal to a provincial court as specified in the applicable provincial assessment legislation.

Grants-in-Lieu

The Canadian Constitution provides that all Crown lands and property are exempt from taxation. In recognition of the cost of providing services to federal and provincial property, the upper levels of government have each adopted their own system of making payments to compensate in whole or part for the loss of taxes that would be payable if the properties were not exempt. These grants are not in all cases the equivalent of full tax; indeed there are categories of Crown property that are not included under such federal or provincial grant arrangements. Federal grants-in-lieu of property tax are generally calculated so that the size of the grant would equal the amount payable if it were taxable property. Urban parklands, Indian reserves and structures such as canal locks, jetties and airport runways are excluded.

Provincial crown corporations in the provinces have individual criteria for making grants-in-lieu. In New Brunswick, all Crown agencies and corporations are subject to full taxes. In Nova Scotia there is a variety of formulae specified in the relevant statutes. In Prince Edward Island, all provincial property situated within a municipality, with the exception of schools and public parks, is subject to municipal taxes. When it is difficult or impractical to arrive at assessed values for some kinds of property, other means must be found to provide an indication of what would be appropriate compensation when public property is exempt from tax.

User Fees

When users of specific services can be identified and their volume of use is measurable, user fees may replace taxation as an alternative method of paying for the service. Examples include admission fees for municipal swimming pools and rinks; metered water rates; parking meters; transit fares; and water hydrant charges. Whether a particular municipal service is to be paid for through a general tax rate, a user fee, or a combination of both, is the kind of financial policy decision that deserves careful consideration by municipal councillors.

The main argument in favour of user fees is that they tend to rationalize the use of municipal services. Only residents willing to pay the fee will demand the service, thereby limiting it to those who really want or need it. Proponents explain that this makes services self-supporting and therefore fairer for all tax payers.

Not everyone accepts that user fees are necessarily fair. Critics note that their imposition may act as a barrier to some individuals or groups in society. If water and sewer were financed entirely through user fees, for example, lower income members of the community would be severely disadvantaged. Likewise, charging for use of recreational facilities would discriminate against poorer children by limiting their access to community parks and playgrounds. Many would argue that it is a basic principle of democratic society that government involvement in service delivery insures the very equality of access that user fees may well inhibit.

Traditionally, user fees have not accounted for a large proportion of municipal revenues; usually in the low single digits. With the current financial plight of many municipalities, however, user fees are frequently championed as an alternative to increases in the general tax rate.

Fines, Licences, and Permits

Fines levied for infractions of municipal by-laws are intended primarily to deter people from breaking the law. Nevertheless, some jurisdictions look at fines, particularly for parking offences, as desirable supplementary revenue. What is often overlooked is the reality that cost of enforcement and collection often exceeds the yield.

Monies collected for regulatory purposes may be considered as a form of revenue generation, although this aspect may be only a secondary consideration. Animal licences, building permits, and licences for tradespeople are common examples of such fees. In larger municipalities, parking fees and building permit fees may be important supports towards the cost of the service provided by the regulating department.

Sale of Services

Revenues collected from the rental of municipal lands, facilities, and equipment; from registration fees for municipal conferences and seminars; from the sale and upkeep of municipal cemetery lots; and from the sale of municipal computer time, are examples of this type of revenue.

Grants

After property taxes, grants are the second most important source of municipal revenue. They primarily involve transfers from the provincial government and are usually classified as either conditional or unconditional.

Unfortunately, the ability of any municipal unit to collect taxes is not necessarily related to the need for its municipal services. A community with declining industry and an aging population may require a high level of service, but the ability of its taxpayers to support costs through property taxes may be inadequate to maintain even a basic level. On the other hand, a rapidly growing residential suburb may require substantial expenditures for recreational facilities and programs, fire and police protective services, residential streets and sidewalks and so on, but lack the commercial and industrial property tax base to help pay costs. In recognition of both such situations, the provinces have been prepared to provide grants to those municipalities without a sufficient tax base to meet the needs from their own resources. Such grants are intended to help provide a uniform service level of municipal services throughout the province.

Conditional Grants

Conditional grants from a province to its municipalities are most often intended for specified capital purposes and, accordingly, have certain conditions attached. Such conditions usually spell out requirements for a specific program or project and often require the receiving municipality to meet some stated proportion of the cost. In accepting a conditional grant, council is bound to accept the conditions attached to it. If the condition is for matching municipal funding, the grant might well limit council's ability to pursue its own agenda.

Municipal governments have, understandably, often been eager to accept conditional grants from senior levels of government. This zeal has consequently obscured the potential distortion or skewing of local priorities. Another risk of tying into a long-term commitment is the danger that several years later, a shift in provincial priorities may alter or eliminate the grant, leaving the municipality with costly administrative infrastructure and a citizenry that has grown accustomed to the service. The danger here is that there is no guarantee that a particular grant program, once started, will be continued.

In former times in Nova Scotia, conditional grants made up a substantial part of municipal revenues. In 1978, for example, grants earmarked specifically in support of education, social services, environment, recreation and culture, protection, transportation, and other services made up more than 50% of the total of all municipal expenditures. As many of these services passed out of municipal control, however, their accompanying grants were likewise withdrawn. With the service exchange program initiated in 1993, conditional grants for operational purposes largely disappeared.

In both Prince Edward Island and New Brunswick the grants that may be considered conditional are those directed towards capital projects such as water and sewer upgrading, infrastructure programs, and community improvement grants.

Unconditional Grants

A conditional grant from a province is designed to reinforce the ability and willingness of a municipal unit to deliver a specific service at a provincially-determined standard. In recent years, however, local governments have lobbied to have grants made without restrictions, so that councils would be free to decide how these monies are spent. Provinces have, by now, generally accepted that local governments may, after all, be in the best position to determine the wants of their citizens, and they have made most municipal grants unconditional. Monies may then be used to supplement overall financial resources of municipalities, allowing local councils to decide the ultimate use of these grants. A particular council may, for example, decide to reduce the pressures on the local property tax, while another may decide to use the grant to provide services not otherwise feasible. Unconditional transfers have thus become a common means of redressing the relative fiscal imbalances among municipalities. In other words, a municipality with a weak fiscal capacity would normally receive a higher per capita grant than a municipality with a strong tax base.

Revenue by Source

Below are three pie charts which graphically depict the sources of revenue for municipalities in each of the three Maritime provinces.

Nova Scotia

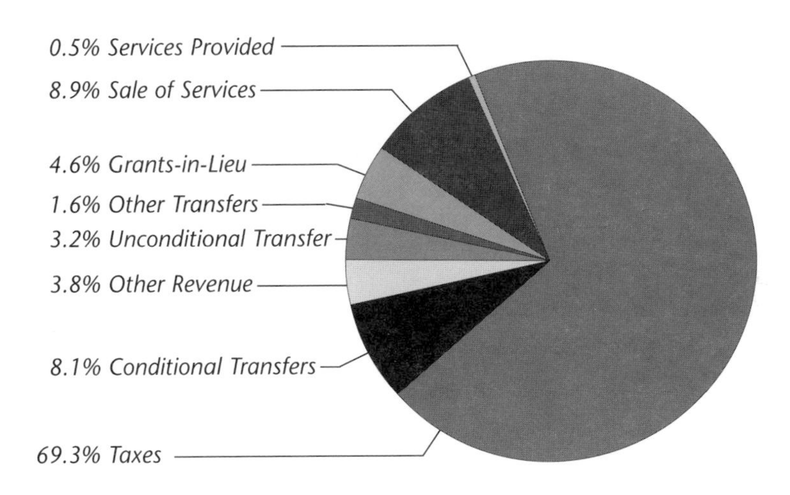

New Brunswick

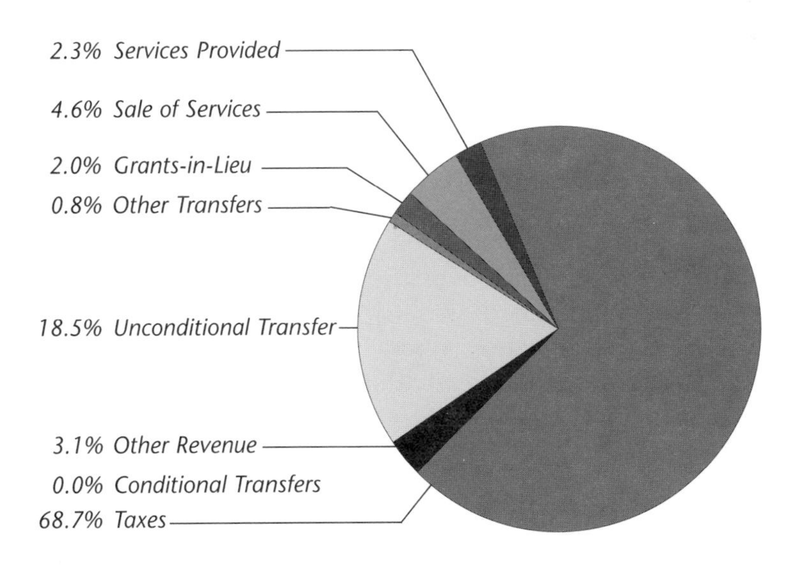

Prince Edward Island

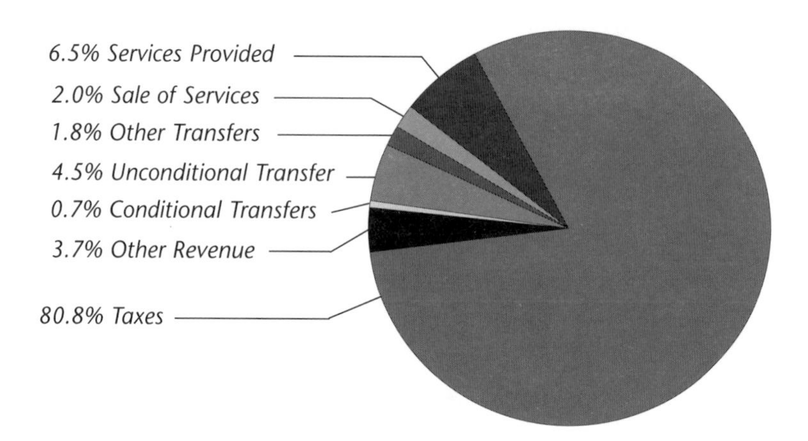

Budgeting

The Operating Budget

The operating budget is the document which identifies the municipality's revenue and expenditure plans for the fiscal year. It is through the operating budget process that council is able to establish its annual tax rates. Once having identified a desired level of services and after having accounted for revenue from other sources, the remainder is what has to be collected in the form of property taxes. It may sound simple, but in practice the process is often a long and complex task. It is not uncommon for councils to review their budget over and over, seeking continually to strike an elusive balance between holding the line on taxes while maintaining an acceptable range and level of services.[3]

The process by which the budget is developed is a key function in any municipality. There needs to be a firm schedule or timetable for preparing the budget document. This schedule should include, among other things, a listing of the groups and individuals who must participate in decisions during the various stages of budget formulation.

Citizens who are interested in learning about, or participating in, the budget process in their municipality should seek out the official with primary responsibility for finances. This person may have a different title in each municipality. In smaller units, it may be the Municipal Clerk or the Deputy Clerk, or even the Chair of the Finance Committee of Council. In

3 In Chapter VIII, we discuss the budget process as a major step in planning. In this chapter we deal with budgeting techniques and with the accounting aspects of the process.

larger units, the person may be the CAO, the Treasurer or the Director of Finance, or the Chief Accountant. Whatever the title, the person should welcome the interest of citizens in the budget process, although at the time that the budget is wending its way through council, time for dialogue with citizens may be at a premium. In general, though, municipal officials are interested in providing an opportunity for individuals and community groups to ask questions, to offer suggestions, and to make their wishes known.

The Capital Budget

In addition to meeting its ongoing operating expenses, municipal government must undertake to pay for required capital projects and assets. A capital asset is any municipal property that has a useful life that exceeds one year. While a pencil might, in the strictest of terms, qualify as a capital asset, in reality the term refers to more substantial items like buildings, land, and major equipment. These acquisitions require outlays that may be too large to be financed through the operating budget. The alternative is to raise the necessary funds through borrowing. The capital budget is the vehicle through which major capital planning and capital acquisition takes place.

Borrowing to finance capital assets is often undertaken with the rationale of aligning the repayment period with the useful life of the asset. In this way there is a matching of benefits and costs over the life of the asset. There are alternative approaches, but some of these may introduce questions of equity. To pay for a major capital asset out of an operating budget would mean that current taxpayers would incur the cost while benefits would continue, without cost, to future taxpayers. On the other hand, to finance the asset beyond its useful life would mean that future taxpayers would pay for an asset that has ceased to produce benefit. These examples may be an oversimplification, nevertheless they illustrate important considerations in capital financing.

A highly responsible method of financing routine replacement of capital equipment without having to borrow is to set up a capital reserve fund. The amount of funds required over a specified period is estimated and annual allocations are made from the operating budget. There are no serious equity problems with this approach and there is the major advantage of savings on interest. This approach is a sign of strong management and a commitment to sound financial planning.

A few municipalities have adopted a pay-as-you go approach to capital financing. Before amalgamation, the former City of Halifax had adopted the practice of paying for capital assets out of the operating budget. There are no serious equity issues with this method of capital financing as long as it continues year after year with roughly the same annual allocation.

Regardless of how they are financed, capital budgets should be based on a realistic projection of future needs and ability to pay for the succeeding five-year period. Most capital improvements, such as servicing of land for future development or the addition of a fire truck, can be forecast well in advance. The capital budget, while prepared or revised annually, should assign priorities to municipal needs and indicate the expected target dates for meeting them.

Capital budgets are generally closely monitored by provincial governments to ensure that municipalities do not incur excessive debt loads. Indeed, in many provinces, borrowing for capital purposes requires approval by the department responsible for municipal affairs or by a designated agency. In New Brunswick such funding is approved by the Municipal Capital Borrowing Board and in Nova Scotia by the Municipal Finance Corporation.

Relationship Between Operating and Capital Budgets

The capital budget has a potential effect on the operating budget in two ways. First, interest on borrowed funds and repayment installments must be included in the yearly operating budget. If municipalities acted with the same abandon that senior governments displayed in the 1970's and 80's, interest from capital borrowing could soon have been consuming a major share of their operating budgets. To limit this possibility, the provinces have imposed policy directions that must be followed by their municipalities. As a result, local governments have generally been quite responsible in living within the prescribed debt ceilings.

A second, and less obvious, effect on the operating budget results from ongoing and unforseen costs in the upkeep of capital assets. Operating expenses of new facilities such as a swimming pool or a hockey rink have often been under-estimated prior to their opening, while recoveries from grants, admissions and user fees may have been over-estimated. Any miscalculations of this sort, unfortunately, will have to be borne by the operating budget.

Political Aspects of Budgeting

The technical aspects of budgeting may not be excessively difficult to master and are usually well understood by municipal staff. The politics of budgeting, however, is a far more complex subject, since it involves the allocation of scarce resources. The question of "who gets what" is at the heart of the municipal politician's role, and is closely linked to the hopes and expectations of citizens in the community. The elected councillors must ultimately make choices about the nature and level of services and must be prepared to strike a balance between the services the community would like to have and its ability to pay for them. It is through the budget that these decisions are made and the municipal politicians will need to work effectively as a team. It means engaging in a continuing dialogue with diverse and sometimes competing community groups while looking to the professional municipal staff for policy advice.

The Budget and Council-Staff Interaction

Budget preparation involves planning by both staff and council. Preparation and management of the budget requires the experience and judgement of both. Experience is important, for the budget must take account of how the municipal unit has operated in previous years. Perhaps experience indicates that some services should be increased, while the need for others has become less important or has disappeared.

Judgement must be used to translate experience into sound decisions. How much can the municipal unit afford to spend on meeting demands for new services? Can increased revenues be expected to exceed the costs of such services, or will a tax increase be required? Are citizens prepared to accept a greater tax load in order to finance improvements in the community? If choices have to be made, which will produce the greater benefit?

Council and staff will need to work closely together in the budget process. Staff will be mainly responsible for bringing the necessary information before council. Staff will also contribute their judgement on what priorities are important. Their viewpoint will tend to focus on the internal needs of the municipal administration; for example, what may be required to maintain the road system in an efficient and up-to-date condition. The councillors for their part must balance the need for an efficient road system against pressure to keep taxes from rising too sharply.

Thus, conflict between staff and council viewpoints is not only possible but is often inevitable at budget time. Such conflict may be seen as a healthy expression of the working of democratic processes, since it forces both sides to look beyond their own immediate concerns. Ultimately, elected councillors must make the decisions, but in the process they must carefully weigh the advice of staff and, at the same time, listen to the various voices from the public they serve.

Preparation for Budgeting

The initial stage of the budget process involves considerable staff effort in assembling information and working out programs, personnel and equipment requirements, and developing cost estimates. This preliminary work requires detailed consultation among department heads, the treasurer, and the clerk or chief administrative officer. In smaller units, the main part of this work is carried out by the clerk-treasurer and from the outset will often involve informal discussion with council members.

When the staff estimates are ready, these are presented to council, which may be sitting as a budget or finance committee. The estimates may be modified or approved by the committee, but the final budget document must be approved by council in regular, open sessions.

Council's Budget Deliberations

The entire budget process provides an opportunity for detailed examination of the total operations of the municipal unit. Councillors have the right to question, to assess, and to press for alternate measures or improvements. Differences of approaches by individual councillors may emerge. Such differences may concern particular programs and departments, or the "fairness" with which different districts or wards are treated. Some councillors may place spending restraints at the top of their priority list, while others may favour increased spending in the interest of what they believe is best for the community. At the same time, the public, in the form of individuals or represented in special interest groups, may be following deliberations and seeking to make their priorities and viewpoints known.

Much study and discussion may be required in order to resolve conflict and reach decisions. Often the early part of the budget debate tends to be more detailed and time-consuming, while in the later stages council may tend to give less careful and systematic scrutiny to individual budget items. While this may be a very human reaction, councillors should consciously attempt to give equally close attention to every budget item.

Expenditures - Budget Flexibility

A municipal budget contains a number of expenditure items that appear to be "locked-in", over which council has little or no room for cost cutting. Such items include mandatory services with standards set by provincial legislation or regulation; services that are provided in accordance with agreements with neighbouring municipal units; and services where contractual cost are involved, including both private corporation agreements as well as collective agreements with unionized employees. In such cases, expenditure obligations may be fixed over a period of years. A similar constraint exists with respect to capital borrowing costs, where interest rates remain fixed for the life of debenture issues.

Many budget expenditures leave little room for council discretion because of decisions in earlier years. For example, capital borrowing may impose a long-range commitment to yearly interest and principal repayments. A major capital work, such as a new water or sewage plant, will establish a minimum annual operating cost many years into the future; therefore, councillors must look particularly closely at the long-term effects of all projects. Debt service charges reflect long-term, fixed commitments. But note the unpredictable commitment that may arise if borrowing has been contracted in a foreign currency that is subject to exchange rate fluctuations.

Innovations in Budget Techniques

Budget preparation is at the heart of all decisions on how to allocate scarce resources to programs competing for attention. There have been various attempts to simplify the process so that the required decisions will reflect sound planning. These attempts have in common the aim of putting the elected representative more directly in charge of decision making.

A budget that provides a specified percentage increase or decrease "across-the-board" leaves little discretion for decision making except in specifying the percentage. The traditional "line-item" budget tends to encourage this kind of approach. Only by considerable digging and questioning can a council member find out what result may be expected from any particular budget expenditure.

A "program-budget", on the other hand, is an attempt to identify the kinds of "output", or services, that a particular allocation of funds can be expected to provide. Thus an expenditure program directed to "fixing potholes" will not only specify the dollar amount, but will also indicate how many miles of road will be looked after with the funding proposed.

"Zero-base" budgets are a further development of program budgeting. In this case, expenditures are listed in program segments. Staff cost each program, specify the expected level of service to be achieved, and arrange the total budget with all the items arranged in order of suggested priority. Council may rearrange some of the priorities, but must also decide the dollar level of the total list. Programs that do not fall above the dollar cut-off point are eliminated.

These different approaches to budgeting suggest some of the alternate methods in how financial planning decisions are made. Council first has to know what kind of information it wants before it chooses how the budget is to be developed, recorded, and reported. The final document represents authorization for staff to implement the financial plan: the *budget.* It also serves to inform the public of the provisions being made for the delivery of municipal services in the fiscal year.

The Budget as a Financial Management Tool

As we have seen, the budget is a plan stated in financial terms. It is an ultimate product of council decision making, but its development involves many actors over a period of time. Once the budget is settled and a tax rate struck, the budget process enters a new phase. While there is a tendency on the part of some councils to think only of the budget as an annual event, nothing could be further from reality.

The budget is a plan and like most plans it tries to anticipate the future with some degree of accuracy. Unfortunately, the future rarely unfolds exactly as one would have anticipated. This is a natural event and inherent in the process of planning. When planning we generally have good information but not perfect information. For example, will the conclusion of collective bargaining result in higher or lower than expected costs? Will there be unscheduled repairs to municipal buildings? Will there be a higher than usual snowfall and will there be changes in provincial transfers to municipalities? These and similar issues illustrate the potential causes that may play havoc with any municipal budget.

Regular budget feedback is a necessary means for councils to determine what, if any, remedial action may be necessary and to maintain reasonable control of what is happening to municipal programs and services. This feedback should come, primarily, from the municipal staff and should be regular and comprehensive in nature.

Auditors and the Audit Report

The dictionary definition of the word auditor is a "person authorized to examine and verify accounts". In modern organizations, whether private or public, the term has come to have a much wider meaning. This can be seen in the work of federal or provincial "auditors general" whose mandates go far beyond merely verifying bookkeeping honesty and mathematical accuracy.

The annual reports of these officials are often a lengthy (and politically embarrassing) chronicle of examples of poor management, unauthorized transactions, wasteful duplication, and inefficient procedures. The emphasis of this approach is on accountability, a term that can be defined as "the obligation to carry out and to respond to a responsibility that has been conferred or delegated". This has introduced the concept of the comprehensive audit, which, in addition to the accounting function, also looks at the entire range of administrative procedures followed within an organization.

At the municipal level, audits still consist largely of a traditional examination of financial records. Some of the larger municipalities may have an internal auditor, whose job is to monitor the operations and transactions of the municipal administration and its various boards, agencies, and commissions. The internal auditor usually acts as a watchdog for the chief administrative officer.

All municipalities must have an external auditor. The external auditor's role is quite simply to report to council on the financial statements prepared by their officials.

A better understanding of the external auditor's role may be obtained by looking at the concept of accountability. As we have noted, in municipal government it is council which has the ultimate responsibility of allocating the funds to provide municipal services to citizens. Administrators, as agents of council, must ensure that these funds are used for the purposes intended. The staff organization must record details of such expenditures using accepted accounting practices. The auditor reports to council, citizens and senior levels of government on how adequately these various requirements have been met. The auditor's statement thus comprises a formal accountability report.

Summary

Growth in demand for municipal services in the Maritimes is commonly seen as outstripping the ability of municipal units to raise revenues to pay for this growth. The resulting fiscal gap has, to varying degrees, been a contributing factor in provincial programs of municipal reform.

The first part of this chapter has examined revenue sources available to the local level, starting with own source revenues: property tax, grants-in-lieu, user fees, fines, licences, and other miscellaneous charges. The next section has dealt with transfers from the provinces in the form of conditional and unconditional grants that are intended to promote province-wide availability of local services.

Following the discussion of how local governments are financed, the next topic has dealt with budgets as the principal instruments municipalities use in managing their affairs. Budgets are of two kinds: the Operating Budget and the Capital Budget. These two types are closely related, in that items in the Capital Budget may be financed by borrowing rather than by paying for them out of current taxes, but eventually all costs wind up as a charge against the Operating Budget.

The budget process is at the heart of most decision making in the municipality. Scarce resources are allocated by an often lengthy and difficult process of setting priorities, weighing the needs of one neighbourhood against those of another, or one program against a second of almost equal urgency. At the end of spending decisions comes an equally painful process of setting tax rates, when councillors must determine the portion to be levied on commercial properties versus those to be imposed on residential owners.

Financial management carries with it accountability responsibilities. Citizens, as well as senior levels of government, need to be provided with accounting information that indicates that the intended services have been adequately delivered, that proper controls are in place, and that prescribed procedures have been followed. It is here that audits and the auditing process provide outside monitoring as added protection for the public interest.

Planning in the Community

The future is too precious to be left entirely to chance.

Introduction

In daily life, everyone "plans". In our work we decide what tasks need to be done first. We plan our leisure time to give us the best return in terms of the things we like to do. We work out our personal finances, making such decisions as whether we can afford to buy a car or take a vacation. We plan for the future in making provision for the education of our children, or in putting savings aside in retirement plans. There are hundreds of examples, each of which has one common element: a process of thinking ahead and making decisions.

Municipalities must plan in a variety of ways, some being more obvious than others.

Policy planning is the basic approach that includes every aspect of the municipal operation. The idea that this type of comprehensive planning may be essential is only just starting to sink in. While individual policies may deal with a variety of public services such as recreation, economic development, road maintenance and many other municipal activities, the integration and assigning of priorities to such diverse needs is not always an easy task. This is where longer range comprehensive planning may create order out of seeming chaos.

The budget process is another form of planning that overlaps with policy planning. This is a mandatory activity that councillors must undertake every year, but it is not always recognized as planning. Wrestling with expenditures, searching for revenues, weighing priorities, the tax burden looming as a dark cloud, they must try to visualize the effect of their decisions on the life of their communities. The operational budget is only the beginning, the capital budget comes next. What major projects are essential for maintaining a healthy community, for ensuring safety and security, for creating economic opportunities?

These are all planning issues and they are central to the budget process. In spite of this close relationship, the idea of a budget as a planning instrument is sometimes overlooked. So a reminder of this fact may not be out of place.[1]

A more familiar planning example is land use planning, which involves decisions about where different elements of the community are to be physically located. Somewhat more broadly, *community planning* starts with land use, but also includes financial, economic, social, environmental, and political considerations that enter into decisions about the physical layout of the community. If community planning is done well, it can result in an attractive community that provides satisfaction and pride to its residents. Conversely, where planning is haphazard or left solely to market forces, development invariably results in ugly sprawl and frustrated citizens.

A third item of planning remains. It is perhaps self-evident that planning must deal with tomorrow's needs, problems, and demands. But what is not as well appreciated is that "tomorrow" includes not only the day after today, but also the weeks, months, years, and decades that stretch far out in the future. This emphasizes that we owe it to our children and our children's children to include *long-range* planning in today's agenda.

These are the types of planning that citizens should expect from their local governments. It is hardly surprising that some councillors may be overawed by such planning challenges, preferring to react to situations as they arise. The result, unfortunately, is that much of council's attention and energy is too often spent in crisis management, leaving little time for planning tasks more essential to the community's future. We will deal in more detail with each of these planning examples in what follows in this chapter.

Policy Planning

The word policy is frequently used in discussing what governments do, but students often find the term somewhat abstract. Webster's New Ideal Dictionary defines policy as *"a course of action selected in light of given conditions to guide and determine decisions"*.[2] Emphasis on the element of

1 The budget process is discussed in greater detail under Municipal Finance in Chapter VII.
2 Webster's New Ideal Dictionary. G.&C. Merriam Co., 1978.

choice occurs in the simpler definition that policy is *"whatever governments choose to do or not to do"*.[3]

Policy planning suggests a rational process of setting objectives and goals designed to guide future council decision making. It starts with the questions "where do we want to go?" and "what are the priorities?" well before the council agenda becomes swamped with problems of the day. Such planning requires a very painstaking examination of the kind of future that the community may expect and how municipal involvement may help to make the best use of all possibilities. There will be choices to be made, and there is the ever present need to ensure that citizen participation rights are respected.

Unfortunately, there are many negative examples of how sloppy planning creates problems for a community. Waiting for a crisis before dealing with a difficult issue is not uncommon in municipal affairs. Acting without adequate information about likely consequences is another. Reacting with panic, bowing to narrow special interest pressures, or adopting half-measures, all point to a common tendency of approaching decisions in an ad hoc fashion. With fiscal restraint characteristic of the 90's, an added barrier to good policy planning has been the pressure on councils "to hold the tax rate". All too often this has been an excuse for avoiding decisions necessary for a healthy and attractive community.

There are both opportunities and barriers to be considered in a comprehensive policy planning process. The economic situation; a well educated workforce; transportation and communication networks; cultural climate; presence of natural resources; a well motivated bureaucracy; adequate educational and library facilities; these are likely assets on which to base a planning strategy.

On the other hand, unresolved problems may undermine the future of the community. Loss of the brightest and best to better opportunities elsewhere is perhaps the most serious of these. Others include environmental issues such as industrial pollution; contaminated ground-water; and exhaustion of mineral, forestry, fishery, and agricultural resources. Then there are structural barriers such as industrial obsolescence and transportation and most distressingly, pockets of chronic poverty. All of these barriers need to be addressed in the policy planning process.

On the other hand, council and citizens must remain aware of the political constraints that tend to limit municipal initiatives. When conflicts arise, provincial priorities must take precedence to those of individual municipalities. The limited taxing power of local government is a formi-

3 David R. Morgan. *Managing Urban America.* Belmont: Waddsworth, 1979, quoted in Tindal & Tindal, *Local Government in Canada, Third Edition.* Toronto: McGraw-Hill Ryerson, 1990, p.256.

dable barrier, a reality further complicated by the appetite of the provinces for a growing share of property taxation.

In any long-range policy planning program, respective roles of council and staff are often crucial elements. There is an all-too-familiar tendency for elected members to become enmeshed in administrative details, while senior staff find themselves forced to fill a resulting policy planning vacuum. Another stakeholder in the process—the public—is often overlooked or consulted too late to have any meaningful influence.

The Budget as a Planning Document

The budget is the instrument for the allocation of scarce resources to programs and services. Accordingly, it is council's key task to see it to completion. Through the budget process, council does four things:

- First, it is an opportunity for council to review existing services to determine if they are being delivered effectively and if they are meeting the needs of the community.
- Second, council is able to articulate the overall direction of the municipality: e.g., what are the goals of the community over the next year? over the next five years?
- Third, it gives both direction and authority to the municipal staff to carry out the will of council.
- Fourth, council is able to set the tax rate. Unfortunately, in many municipalities, too much emphasis is placed on setting the tax rate before undergoing a really thorough examination of the budget.

Land Use Planning

Planning involving land use is not a simple process, for there are differing personalities, conflicting interests, and often strongly held attitudes towards property rights. There is usually a municipal or district planning department, but other departments are also involved, including those responsible for public works, environmental services and fire protection, as well as bodies such as the public health commission or the district school board. In addition to municipal concerns, other provincial government departments, public organizations, and individuals may have interests in the planning process.

In the face of this complex of different viewpoints, provincial planning legislation generally aims to establish a viable framework for municipal and provincial land use planning. The provincial Acts define the guidelines and the powers that are delegated to municipal councils in community planning matters. Planning programs may often give rise to controversy and therefore offer challenges to every councillor, but the benefits to be achieved from informed and thoughtful effort are well worth the time and energy that land use planning demands.

Common Planning Problems

At almost every meeting, councils are faced with decisions related to development in their municipalities. A council with an effective planning program can deal with these situations in an efficient, rational manner. Without this, a wide range of problems can arise. The examples listed below are typical:

Land Use Conflicts: Where development takes place without direction, it is easy to see the results: industries locating in the middle of residential areas, highways with traffic problems due to commercial sprawl, and mixtures of incompatible and unattractive buildings. Helter-skelter development lowers property values and makes a community less desirable as a place to live and work.

Loss of Natural Resources: Unplanned development can result in contamination of water supply areas or depletion of groundwater, loss of prime recreational or agricultural land, and other environmental damage.

More Expensive Services: When development occurs in an unplanned, scattered manner, sewer and water lines may have to be extended prematurely or needlessly; there may have to be either more schools or longer bussing routes; and services such as roads, fire and police protection, street lighting, and recreation facilities are likely to be more expensive for the municipal taxpayer.

Insufficient Services: Without adequate planning, land necessary for schools and recreational areas may not be available, access to undeveloped land may be blocked, and transportation facilities may be inadequate or strangled by bottlenecks. Some services may be overburdened while others have excess capacity.

Such examples show the direct relationship between land use and financial issues. In the current economic climate, councils must be even more alert in making decisions which maximize benefits and avoid waste.

Such decisions, of course, depend on access to the kind of information that is crucial for effective planning.

Planning in Your Municipality

If your municipality does not have a municipal plan and land use zoning by-law (to be discussed later in this chapter), how would the following situations be handled in your municipal unit?

- A request from a developer to extend the municipal sewer lines to service a proposed subdivision.
- A proposal to build a shopping centre in the municipality.
- A petition from a neighbourhood group to deal with a traffic problem in their area.
- A request to the municipality to pave a certain street.
- A request to the municipality to take over a private road.
- A proposal to establish a 100-unit mobile home park in the municipality.
- A request to site a mobile home on a particular lot.

It may come as a surprise to most residents and even to many council members that in the absence of planning controls, the municipality would have no control over the outcome of most of the items in the above list. If your municipal unit has a proper planning process and effective by-laws in place, most of these issues would probably have been addressed and the mechanism to deal with them will already be in place. If this is not the case in your community, read on!

Land Use Planning Framework

Provincial planning legislation enables municipalities to guide and control development through the adoption of municipal planning strategies and land use or zoning by-laws. Through by-laws and regulations, councils are able to control subdivision practices in an orderly manner. In addition to development control, planning legislation provides the means to co-ordinate the provision of services, transportation improvements, and community facilities.

To provide for broader input into planning decisions, municipalities often establish a Planning Advisory Committee (PAC). Two primary roles of the PAC are the advisory and adjustment functions. While such a committee may not be mandatory, it is obviously a highly desirable means for securing community involvement in the planning process. To have credibility, a PAC must include both councillors and members of the public. Some councils follow the practice of involving every councillor on the PAC together with citizens, on the theory that planning is at the heart of most council activities. Other councils have opted for a smaller PAC, in the expectation that fewer members will make for more efficient work.

The role of the PAC is to advise council on matters related to land use planning. It is intended that it advise principally on policy questions, rather than on the daily administration of planning controls, such as bylaws and regulations. The latter are the work of planning staff, and should occupy PAC or the full council only in cases where unforeseen problems arise or policy decisions are required.

Municipal Planning Strategy

The terms "municipal planning strategy" or the "municipal plan" both describe the series of policies which have been adopted to guide all future development in a municipality. The term "planning strategy" is used in Nova Scotia planning legislation while New Brunswick and Prince Edward Island use the simpler term. Under either name, the statement of policies must be based on detailed studies of planning problems and issues that may exist in the community. This type of background will provide the basis for decisions on matters such as areas for future residential, commercial and industrial development, required park and recreation areas, natural resource conservation, and other matters that may be specified in provincial Acts. Once such policies are adopted, they form the framework for future council decisions on development matters. By acting in accordance with established policies set forth in the strategy, problems that usually result from ad hoc decisions are less likely to occur.

The municipal planning strategy[4] also serves as a guideline for location and provision of sewer, water, health, schools, recreation and other community facilities and helps in assessing programs and funding needs. The strategy should relate such programs directly to the financial capabilities of the municipality and thus provide council with direction for decisions relating to capital expenditures and in assigning priorities to competing needs. It should allow for flexibility, since changes in circum-

4 For "municipal planning strategy", also read "municipal plan".

stances such as interest rate changes, cost-sharing programs, and other economic factors may require a reordering of priorities.

In New Brunswick, a series of District Planning Commissions and a Rural Planning District Commission provide land use planning services to municipal councils and to Rural Community Committees in unincorporated areas. These services cover development of municipal and rural plans, and help in the drafting, adoption, and enforcement of planning by-laws and regulations. District Commissions also offer building inspection services in unincorporated areas and by agreement in municipalities.

There are several methods by which a municipal council can prepare its municipal planning strategy. The technical work can be done for the Planning Advisory Committee by professional planners on the municipal staff, by consultants, or planners employed by a District Planning Commission. Experience in all provinces has shown that the best approach involves broad interaction between professional planners, the Planning Advisory Committee, and members of the public.

Legislation generally sets out required procedures for adoption of a municipal planning strategy. In all three provinces, planning strategies must include policies necessary to carry out the intent of applicable provincial land use policies and must be approved by the Minister responsible for municipal affairs before they come into effect. Provincial planners are normally available to assist the municipal staff in preparing the various components. This advisory service may be important in the early identification and possible solution of problems arising during plan preparation.

Provincial planning legislation requires that citizens have access to the municipal planning process, so that interested individuals and groups may make their views and concerns known before the formal planning document is adopted. To ensure that such access is meaningful, councils must make known how public participation will be provided before the process gets underway.

In summary, the municipal planning strategy contains a statement of council's policy intent for the future development of the municipality, providing a framework for the delivery of services, and presenting a map of the desired future land use pattern of the municipality. The strategy is oriented towards solving existing problems and working towards the desired future form of the municipality. Most planning legislation in Canada requires councils to review an existing municipal plan or strategy at intervals of not more than five years.

Land Use (or Zoning) By-Laws

The municipal planning strategy is usually a general set of statements of policy. In contrast, a land use or zoning by-law is very specific. The strategy deals with overall policies and the latter deals with the specific development standards to implement land use policies. The land use by-law is a working instrument intended to ensure that development in the municipality occurs in the pattern which council has chosen in its municipal planning strategy. It thereby allows council to monitor and control future growth.

The land use by-law brings in the concept of zoning. In zoning, the community is divided into various districts, or zones, such as residential, commercial and industrial, institutional, agricultural, park and open space. Such zoning is the means for carrying out the intent of the municipal planning strategy. The land use by-law (in New Brunswick called zoning by-law) may have regulations to include:

- use of lands, buildings and structures;
- development agreements;
- density of population;
- amount of open space;
- percentage of a lot that may be covered by structures;
- size and heights of buildings;
- parking and loading space requirements;
- front, rear, and side yard requirements;
- hazard lands;
- signs and advertisement; and
- various other standards which will allow council to meet its land use policies.

That the land use by-law and the municipal planning strategy are very closely related may be illustrated in two ways:

1. A land use by-law must be consistent with the municipal planning strategy. This is to ensure that the by-law is based on

agreed-upon policies, making it more likely to be upheld if challenged before a provincial planning tribunal or in the courts.

2. Council must adopt a zoning plan and land use by-law concurrently with a municipal planning strategy, as this by-law is the major means for implementing the plan.

Land use by-laws are legally enforceable documents and affect individual rights in land, and therefore must be based upon legally valid criteria and accepted planning principles. This means that a municipal planning strategy must very clearly provide policies and background information indicating why parcels of land are treated in a certain manner in a land use by-law.

Zoning or land use by-laws that are based on the municipal planning strategy, that are rational, and that enjoy community support, will be far more successful than attempts by council to deal with new situations according to which group can generate the most pressure. There will always be some element of lobbying, but council will be in a better position to act responsibly if there is in place a carefully developed plan and corresponding land use by-law.

In New Brunswick, an innovative new planning instrument in the form of a Rural Plan was introduced to facilitate management of land use planning issues in villages and unincorporated areas. Essentially it combines policy statements with zoning standards into a single document.

Provincial Subdivision Regulations

To provide uniformity, provincial governments have uniform sets of regulations governing subdivision of land. The purpose of such regulations is to provide rules, standards, and procedures for the subdivision of land. They generally set out requirements such as minimum lot areas, frontages, and approvals from departments of health and transportation. The regulations may include:

- procedures for submitting tentative and final plans of subdivision;

- information requirements for tentative and final plans;

- referral of plans to other departments for specific approval (such as health and environment) and in rural areas, applications for percolation tests and permits to install on-site sewage disposal systems;

- in rural municipalities, referral of plans to the engineering section of the provincial highway or roads department for approval of streets and roads;

- fees to be charged for the registration of plans of subdivision;

- minimum lot sizes and frontages (if not covered in a land use by-law); and

- provision for limiting the number of lots that can be subdivided from a plan where lots are not serviced by a public street or road.

Such provincial regulations may be specified for all or part of the province, or may contain different requirements for different parts of the province.

Municipal Subdivision By-Laws

Where provincial subdivision regulations have been prescribed, a municipal council may adopt its own supplementary subdivision by-law. This affords council further control over development, as it may include:

- standards for the construction and installation of water services, sanitary and storm sewers;

- areas to be reserved for public purposes;

- regulations concerning minimum lot frontages and building lines, and the size and shape of blocks and lots;

- regulations governing subdivision of lands fronting on lakes and waterways;

- in the case of a city or incorporated town, standards and requirements for the construction, width, gradients and location of streets and roads, and the widening and modification of existing streets and roads;

• requirements for subdividers in installing water and sewer services and the construction, lay out, grading, and paving of any proposed street in the subdivision, and for performance bonds to ensure that the work is carried out; and

• requirements for subdividers to deed portions of land to the municipality for park or public purposes, or for payment in cash-in-lieu, or for transfer of land of equivalent value on terms acceptable to council.

Other Development Controls

In addition to zoning land use by-laws, subdivision regulations, and subdivision by-laws, there are additional methods by which council can control development. These include by-laws to regulate building standards, mobile home parks, and minimum standards regarding matters such as sanitation and room sizes. In Prince Edward Island there are special provisions governing the acquisition and ownership of land by non-residents of the province. More information on such regulations and by-laws may be obtained from the respective provincial departments responsible for municipal matters.

Development Officer

Upon adoption of a land use by-law, council must appoint a Development Officer and delegate to this person the administrative responsibilities of the by-law. Given a clearly written municipal planning strategy and set of by-laws, the development officer can be expected to carry out the intent of council. He or she is the municipal official responsible for issuing development permits signifying compliance with the land use by-laws.

The development officer provides two major benefits to council:

1. Efficient and uniform administration by a trained, competent employee.

2. Less time spent in PAC and council meetings on administration, leaving councillors more time to deal with policy, long-range planning, and other essential issues.

In unincorporated areas of Prince Edward Island or where there is no municipal subdivision by-law, the development officer may be designated by the Minister. In New Brunswick, the District Planning Commissions provide building inspection services.

District Planning Commissions and Joint Planning Advisory Committees

Various mechanisms have been proposed or established to secure co-operative planning among neighbouring municipalities and to make better use of planning professionals. These include District Planning Commissions, and in Nova Scotia, Joint Planning Advisory Committees, which may be established to serve two or more municipal units. These help to facilitate co-operative planning between neighbouring municipal units.

The Role of Provincial Governments

Departments Responsible for Municipal Affairs

(A) Provincial Land Use Policies and Regulations

Under provincial planning Acts, the Governor-in-Council, (or in effect the Cabinet) has the right to adopt provincial land use policies dealing with the use and protection of the province's land resources, lands subject to erosion, large-scale developments, and the subdivision of lands, to name but a few of the subject areas. Any provincial land use policy may apply to all or part of the province and there may be different policies for different parts of the respective provinces. Where there is no municipal land use by-law in effect, the provincial land use regulations may require that a provincial development permit be obtained prior to initiating particular developments.

(B) Provincial Review of Municipal Planning

In New Brunswick, the Minister responsible for municipal affairs has the power to review and approve all rural plans and municipal plans. In Nova Scotia and Prince Edward Island, the approval requirement extends to land use by-laws and subdivision by-laws. In practice, the review process usually involves a departmental committee that includes planning and legal staff. It has become normal practice to submit draft strategies and by-laws for comment from the Department very early in the preparation process. Ongoing consultation provides opportunities for provincial planners to advise local governments on the government's planning policies and goals.

(C) Financial Assistance for Planning

In the days before severe financial restraint, financial assistance was often available to municipalities to enable them to develop their own planning capability. Such help included cost-sharing in setting up joint or district planning commissions and in preparation and administration of a municipal planning strategy and supporting by-laws. The provincial planning authorities also were able to provide municipalities with professional planners on a temporary basis pending the hiring and training of locally-based staff. A common solution has sometimes been to share staff with neighbouring municipal units through a District Planning Commission. With the emphasis on down-sizing, however, municipalities have had much less access to assistance of this kind.

Departments of Environment

Departments of Environment will generally, upon request, review and comment on any draft municipal planning strategy, subdivision or other development proposal. Such review will identify possible environmental concerns related to water quality, sewage disposal, storm drainage and watercourse alterations. The responsible Minister is empowered to order a public hearing, including a full scale environmental review for major developments or projects.

Public Health Inspection Service

Provincial public health inspectors play a role in planning matters through their responsibility for inspection and approval of on-site septic waste systems. Percolation tests are required to determine the suitability of land for such disposal systems, with provincial standards specifying minimum lot sizes, frontages, set backs, and separation distances. In the case of lots with water frontage, more stringent requirements are demanded.[5]

5 While provincial subdivision regulations cover standards designed to protect development along river and lake frontage, any lots laid out before the adoption of many such regulations are exempt under the grand-fathering principle. The result is that many older subdivisions have no firm standards and could pose potential environmental hazards for wildlife and humans alike.

Planning legislation normally requires that no subdivision in rural municipalities may be approved by a development officer until provincial transportation engineers have approved plans for public streets and roads. Limited development on private roads may be permitted provided that the proposed street right-of-way alignments and gradients are approved. Here again, however, developments on pre-existing private roads may be exempt from such standards.

Planning Appeals

Individuals who consider themselves aggrieved by any decision under planning legislation or regulation have the right to seek redress from the appropriate provincial tribunal or appeals board. Specific grounds for appeal are spelled out in each of the respective provincial planning Acts. Typically, however, decisions of council and staff of the following types may be subject to appeal:

- the approval or refusal of an amendment to the land use by-law;

- the refusal of a subdivision plan under the subdivision regulations or by-laws;

- the refusal to grant a municipal development permit under the land use by-law by the development officer;

- the refusal of a provincial development permit pursuant to provincial land use regulations; and

- the approval or refusal by council to enter into a development agreement.

Where the appeal is from a decision of council, the appeal tribunal will not interfere unless it can be shown that the decision is inconsistent with the planning strategy document or land use by-law on which the decision is based.

Land Use Planning Summary

Planning legislation provides for both provincial and municipal involvement in guiding and regulating land development. Provincial land use policies and regulations are intended to help ensure the protection of the land resources and envisage an orderly system of land subdivision. Municipal units, however, are given the primary authority for planning within their respective jurisdictions through the drafting and adoption of municipal planning strategies, land use or zoning by-laws, and subdivision by-laws. Within this framework, the development officer has overall responsibility for implementation. Public participation is an important element in the entire land use planning process, and councils must ensure a fair and efficient administrative system.

While the Maritime region as a whole is not experiencing extreme growth pressures, many parts of all three provinces are undergoing significant changes. Sporadic growth may easily damage a fragile natural environment, the character of a small town, or the appearance of a rural area. Past neglect of land use planning, environmental abuse, or lack of resources, may all have left a legacy of ugly problems. Past, present, and future problems can only be addressed if both council and citizens are prepared to make effective planning a top community priority.

Strategic (Long-Range) Planning

Rational Planning Model[1]

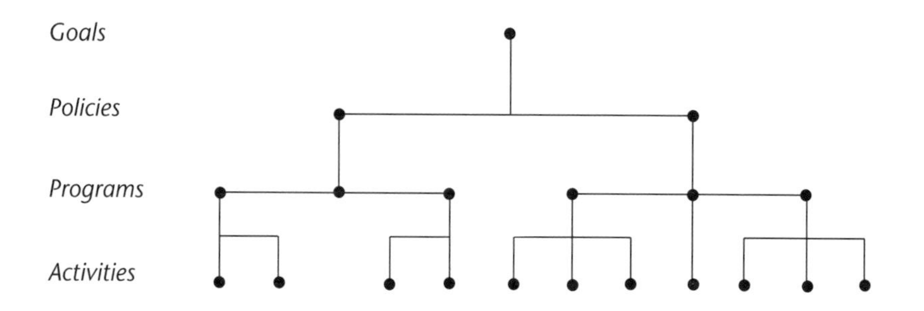

1 John M. Bryson. *Strategic Planning for Public and Non-Pofit Organizations (Revised Edition)*, San Francisco: Jossey Bass Publishers, 1995.

The term "strategic" has come into use as a word to describe a systematic approach wherein the municipality is able to identify its overall direction, build commitment among key stakeholders, sharpen organizational focus and allocate scarce resources. It is a form of rational planning that places emphasis on goals, policies, programs, and activities.

Strategic planning is, essentially, the most recent attempt to develop a comprehensive and rational long-range planning model. There are several advantages to this approach. The first and perhaps most important is the process itself, which encourages municipal officials to think about their municipality and community in a more co-ordinated and focused way. Even if a formal plan does not emerge, the mere act of thinking "strategically" is of great value. This way of thinking can best take place when the daily demands of office routines are temporarily set aside. Accordingly, many organizations make use of retreats as an effective means of launching the strategic planning process.

A further benefit is the actual development of a plan which documents the strategic issues that face the municipality and outlines the ways in which the council and staff plan to respond. The real promise of strategic planning lies in its comprehensive nature. In areas such as economic development, land use and budgeting too often tends to be fragmented and uneven, so here the strategic approach brings them together, placing them into an overall vision of the community's future.

This type of long-range planning is not without drawbacks. Since it is more a way of thinking than a well-defined process, individuals may find

Political Decision-making Model

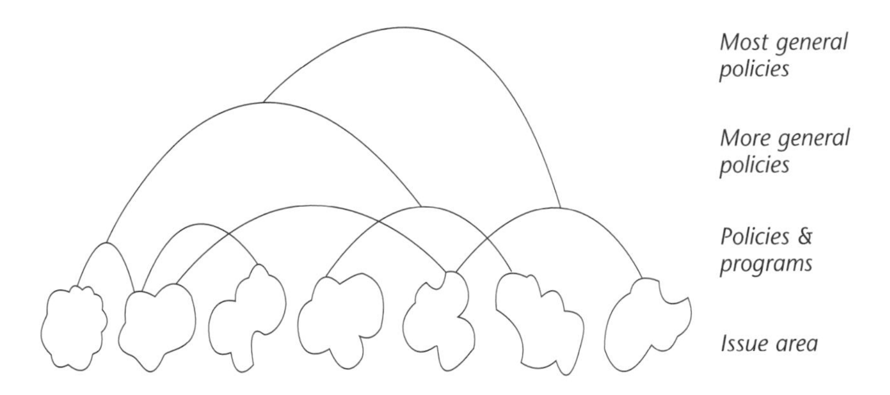

themselves operating beyond their comfort level. Furthermore, it runs counter to the habitual method of tackling problems individually and with "band-aid" solutions. Accordingly, it is not surprising that even with a strategic plan in place, politicians will often follow the more inductive political decision-making model.

For strategic planning to be effective, it must draw upon the strengths of both the rational and political decision-making models. It implies that the plan is a living document which can be amended to accommodate changes as they occur. Too often organizations take what they are already doing and place it within a strategic planning format. This is merely justifying existing programs and services. While it may make the protagonists feel better, it serves little else.

Summary

Planning is a basic concept that ought to pervade all processes of local government. The most essential requirement for adequate planning starts with the policy process. Policy planning involves a systematic approach to decision making. By thinking ahead about possible futures for any municipality, it becomes apparent that how a community evolves is highly dependent on a variety of decisions by its local government. At a basic level, the budget is a plan in financial terms.

Community and land use planning involves conscious decisions about the shape and structure of neighbourhoods and their relationship to location of commercial, industrial, institutional, and recreational facilities in the community. In rural communities, decisions additionally involve issues of renewable resources and environmental protection.

Strategic or long-range planning is a more recent instrument for thinking about and co-ordinating all future oriented activities. It seeks to channel council decision making into a rational approach to the future of the community. When council is too preoccupied with daily problems and has little time to think about the months and years ahead, it is highly likely that the community will develop in a haphazard way. Land use decisions will be left entirely to "market" forces, which inevitably means ugly sprawl. Financial planning will be limited to desperate measures to try to bring in a balanced budget, without too much thought given to long-range needs. But when council commits to planning in all its aspects, it is a policy decision that will provide the best possible future for the municipality and its citizens.

Chapter IX

Operations and Procedures of Municipal Council[1]

Introduction

Who has not vowed, at some time or other, never to attend another meeting? Meetings that start late and drag on without constructive outcome, that drift aimlessly from one topic to another, or where discussion is monopolized from the chair or by some other garrulous speaker, are all too familiar. When such meetings take place in municipal council chambers, tempers and frustrations often cause the business of local government to grind tediously to a halt.

Despite the fact that procedure is central to the fundamental process of municipal decision making, procedure is a subject that often tends to be neglected. If members understand clearly how meetings ought to be conducted, it helps to reduce frustrations and to increase the council's sense of accomplishment. Likewise, citizens will have more confidence in councillors who are able to conduct their affairs in an orderly manner.

This chapter offers an outline of the kinds of procedure that are essential to effective municipal decision making. It is primarily aimed at elected officials in local government, but members of the general public who participate in organizational activities may also find the contents useful.

Legal Framework

As noted in Chapter II, a municipality is a corporation established under authority of the appropriate provincial legislation governing municipal organizations. The statutes themselves do not specify detailed rules for the conduct of municipal council meetings; rather, councils are empowered to adopt, through by-laws, their own procedure.

1 This chapter incorporates a large part of the text prepared by Donald MacLean for earlier editions of *A Guide to Local Government in Nova Scotia.*

Most municipalities follow, at least in theory, standard parliamentary procedure as originally outlined in *Bourinot's Rules of Order.*[2] Adapted properly for use by municipal councils, parliamentary procedure facilitates discussion, participation by individual councillors or aldermen, and the orderly conduct of council business. Council decisions, which relate frequently to complex issues, often require substantial time and care. It is important for each municipal council to seek to run its meetings in a way that will earn public confidence and respect. The public sometimes tends to become impatient with what seems to be a painfully slow process in arriving at decisions. In those instances where faulty procedure needlessly prolongs debate, this dissatisfaction is fully justified.

Councils are empowered to appoint committees (standing committees and special committees), boards, and commissions. Certain municipal committees and boards may be required by provincial statute. All of these bodies are usually set up under by-laws or resolutions specifying composition and procedure. Committees can be an effective way of doing much of the detailed work that allows the regular council meetings to focus on broad policy issues. Boards and commissions likewise allow specialized administrative matters to be dealt with more thoroughly than would be possible within the time available during council meetings.

Meetings

Each municipal council has authority (with certain exceptions covered by provincial legislation) to make by-laws concerning the time and frequency of its own meetings, thus ensuring that council meets on a regular basis and at stated times. These can vary widely from municipality to municipality.

Frequency is influenced by the size of the municipal unit and whether it is urban or rural. Rural municipal councils are usually not required by law to meet as often as those with more sophisticated urban responsibilities, but they have tended in recent years to become just as overburdened as urban municipalities and to meet almost as frequently. Most municipal councils meet regularly at least once a month and in some cases on a bi-weekly or weekly basis.

Provincial legislation requires that meetings of municipal councils, whether urban or rural, be open to the public and that all business conducted become a matter of public information. The spirit of openness does not allow "in camera" meetings of council, but it has become prac-

2 M.K. Kerr and H.W. King. *Procedures for Meetings and Organizations, Third Edition*, 1996. This is a comprehensive and up-to-date manual that incorporates the principles of parliamentary procedure set forth in *Bourinot's Rules of Order.*

tice to refer matters involving confidentiality to a standing or special committee of council, where this prohibition is less explicit. The assumption is that discussion may take place in closed meetings of committees, but binding decisions must be made only in open council meetings.

Councils are also empowered to call *special* meetings. These meetings must be called by formal notice, and within a prescribed time, specifying the business to be transacted. A special meeting of council has no authority to deal with business other than specified in the notice of such meeting. Emergency meetings may also be called on shorter notice.

Quorum

The Latin word *quorum* ("of whom") means the minimum number of members whose presence is necessary for the valid transaction of business. Municipal legislation often stipulates that a quorum of council consists of a simple majority of council members.

Rules of Procedure

Provincial legislation stipulates who shall preside over municipal council meetings. For towns, cities, and regional municipalities, it is the mayor; for villages and other rural municipalities, the title may be chairman or chairperson; in county or district municipalities in Nova Scotia it is "warden". In the absence of mayor, chair or warden, the deputy must preside. Municipal by-laws usually provide for procedure to be followed should any of these officials be absent.

The task of whoever is in the chair is demanding. It is the chairperson's responsibility to ensure that municipal council business is conducted in accordance with appropriate procedure. Each councillor, as well as the chairperson, should study and remain familiar with prescribed procedure; it is exceedingly difficult for a chairperson, however well informed, to conduct a meeting where councillors are ignorant of procedure or fail to appreciate its practical value.

The chairperson should refrain, while in the chair, from expressing personal opinion concerning matters that come before council. Most chairmen discover early that this constraint requires a measure of self-discipline. If a chairperson decides to express personal opinions, he or she must vacate the chair and request the deputy to preside.

The chairperson should have a clear understanding of all issues that are to come before each municipal council meeting, in order that these may be defined with precision and so that discussion remains relevant. At the same time, the chairperson must be sensitive to minority views and insist on their right to be heard.

Agenda

Agenda is a Latin word that means "things to be done". A municipal council's agenda is, therefore, a list of things to be done or an orderly schedule of business. Most municipalities have a by-law concerning agendas. The following is a typical list of items that may appear:

- Opening of meeting
- Minutes of previous meeting
- Business arising from minutes
- Committee reports or resolutions
- Deputations or delegations
- Correspondence
- By-laws
- Motions or notices of motion
- New business
- Adjournment

Preparation of the agenda is often a joint task for the chairperson in co-operation with senior staff. These individuals should spend some time going over the agenda, in advance of the meeting, noting the background information available and becoming familiar with the points on which decisions are to be made.

Every agenda should be circulated in advance and accompanied by copies of relevant reports and other background documents. Longer reports should include an executive summary page for the convenience of councillors who are undoubtedly so "swamped with paper" that they are unable to get through lengthy reports on the spur of the moment. Advance circulation gives individual councillors or other committee members an opportunity to make pertinent preliminary enquiries for additional information.

Minutes

Minutes are the official written record of a council meeting and include the names of all members present. The municipal clerk, who is responsible in each municipality for recording the minutes, is required by law to keep, in the municipal office, an official minute book of all meetings of council and of council committees.

Each official decision of council is recorded in the minutes, although normally a detailed report of debate is not included. It is desirable sometimes to include a summary of discussion related to a particular issue; this is a matter of individual council preference or discretion. Minutes should, however, refer explicitly to reports and recommendations submitted to council, copies of which ought to be kept on file as part of the official record. Unlike provincial and federal legislatures, municipal councils are not required to record complete and verbatim accounts of their proceedings. It may be appropriate, however, to provide for taping of proceedings for possible future reference, thereby simplifying any future questions with regard to the minutes.

Minutes record official decisions and thereby provide an authoritative reference for subsequent action to be taken. Adequate minutes serve, also, as a valuable source of background information and as a record of precedents for future reference and guidance.

Precedence of Motions

It is permissible, when a motion is under consideration, for discussion to be interrupted by the introduction of one or more other motions. The chairperson should know which motions are admissible, at any given time, and which motions are inadmissible. If the chairperson is fully aware of the conventional precedence of motions, personal embarrassment can be avoided and, sometimes, the disarray of council itself. It is a simple matter: the chairperson can either commit to memory the table of precedence, or affix the table to a cardboard kept always well within reach.

If, during discussion of a particular motion, a councillor or alderman seeks to introduce another motion, the chairperson has but to consult the table of precedence. If the new motion is of a kind listed "ahead of" the kind already under discussion, the new motion takes precedence and must be dealt with before council can resume discussion of the earlier motion. Similarly, if the new motion is of a kind listed "after" the motion already under discussion, the new motion does *not* take precedence, and it must not be introduced for discussion at that time.

Table of Precedence

1. Motion to set the time of the next meeting
   .. requires a mover and a seconder
   .. requires, for adoption, a majority vote
   .. may be debated, but only as to the time

2. Motion to set the time to adjourn
   .. requires a mover and a seconder
   .. requires, for adoption, a majority vote
   .. may be debated, but only as to the time of adjournment

3. Motion to adjourn
   .. requires a mover and a seconder
   .. requires, for adoption, a majority vote
   .. may be debated, but only as to the time of adjournment

4. Motion to recess
   .. requires a mover and a seconder
   .. requires a majority vote
   .. must not be debated

5. Motion to raise a question of privilege
   .. requires a mover only, who may interrupt another speaker
   .. requires no vote
   .. must not be debated

6. Motion to raise a point of order
   .. requires a mover only, who may interrupt another speaker
   .. requires no vote
   .. must not be debated

7. Motion to lay on the table *or*
   Motion to remove from the table
   .. requires a mover and a seconder
   .. requires a majority vote
   .. must not be debated

8. Motion to put the previous question
   .. requires a mover and a seconder
   .. requires a two-thirds vote
   .. must not be debated

9. Motion to limit debate *or*
   Motion to extend the limit of debate
   .. requires a mover and a seconder
   .. requires a majority vote
   .. must not be debated

10. Motion to postpone to a definite time
   .. requires a mover and a seconder
   .. requires a majority vote
   .. may be debated, but only as to the time

11. Motion to commit or refer
   (e.g., to a standing committee or to a special committee)
   .. requires a mover and a seconder
   .. requires a majority vote
   .. may be debated

12. Motion to amend
   .. requires a mover and a seconder
   .. requires a majority vote
   .. may be debated

13. The Main Motion
   .. requires a mover and a seconder
   .. requires a majority vote
   .. may be debated

14. Motion to rescind *or*
   Motion to reconsider
   .. is a main motion
   .. requires a mover and a seconder
   .. requires a majority vote, if introduced with advance notice; or, otherwise, a two-thirds vote.

Amendments to Motions

Motions to amend motions often create procedural difficulty, either because the chairperson or councillors are unclear about the defined limitations of motions to amend or because a proposed amendment has been badly worded.

It is essential to remember than an amendment *mends.* A proposed amendment must not *negate* the essential purpose or intent of the motion that it seeks to alter. The purpose of every proper amendment is to modify the main motion so that, when the time comes for council to vote on the main motion, the *wording* of the main motion will have been altered or "improved".

Every amendment alters a motion in one of the following three ways and in no other way:

1. By adding words (insertion).
2. By taking away words (deletion).
3. By taking away words and putting new words in their place (substitution).

A motion to amend should always include one of the following three expressions:

1. ". . that the main motion be amended by inserting the word(s) . ."
2. ". . that the main motion be amended by deleting the word(s) . ."
3. ". . that the main motion be amended by substituting the word(s) . ."

There is no procedural limit to the number of times that a main motion may be amended before it is put to a vote. As soon as one amendment has been voted upon (that is, either adopted, defeated or referred), another amendment may be introduced. At any one time, however, a council must not have before it more than one amendment to an amendment. If amendments to a motion become numerous and cumbersome, it may be preferable to withdraw the main motion and to introduce a new main motion.

Voting

Legislation usually specifies that questions arising in council shall be decided by a majority of votes. The chairperson or mayor normally has a right to vote on all questions before council. In the event of a tie vote, the issue is deemed to have been lost. In some jurisdictions a vote by the mayor is only cast when councillors have reached a tie.[3]

3 It should be noted that under some circumstances, legislation can specify that a specific majority is required. For example, in New Brunswick, the Municipalities Act stipulates that a two-thirds majority vote of council is required in order to dismiss a full-time employee.

Resolutions and By-Laws

Every *adopted* motion is, by definition, a resolution, and municipal council meetings should dispose of all matters (either minor or major) by motion. This is the standard and required procedure, regardless of whether an issue before council relates, for instance, to an additional staff position, a million-dollar capital project, or a proposed new by-law. In practice, a motion (that is, a *proposed* resolution) includes a preliminary statement or preamble ending with the words: "therefore, be it resolved that ...". Motions are the standard device for introducing discussion leading to decisions by which municipal council's authority is exercised.

Municipal by-laws, which are analogous to provincial statutes, are adopted by a process more formal than that used for resolutions. Advance notice of motion to propose adoption of a by-law must be given prior to official consideration by municipal council. It is, indeed, unlawful for a proposed by-law to be discussed by council unless the proposer has given due advance notice of intention to propose. In actual practice, most by-laws are drafted and redrafted through committee work and, when presented to council, are already in a form acceptable for discussion and decision by council. It is for a councillor or alderman proposing to introduce a by-law to take care that it has been drafted properly and that it means in fact exactly what the proposer intends it to mean.

By-laws reflect a municipal council's major policies and are, therefore, an instrument by which fundamental council objectives are realized.

Committees, Boards, and Commissions

Boards and commissions, in some instances, are responsible only in part to the municipal council(s) whose rate-payers they serve. This is true, for instance, of joint expenditure bodies where jurisdiction is shared with other municipal units or shared by both municipal and provincial levels of government. Matters of board and commission accountability may from time to time raise contentious problems for municipal councils.

The *standing* committees of a municipal council (its permanent committees) generally relate to finance, public works, by-law amendments, and to other central concerns of council. It is at the standing committee level that many matters are given careful and detailed scrutiny before they are referred, for formal decision, to council itself. Increasingly, however, standing committees are being replaced by the council "committee of the whole" system. This provides opportunity for all members of council to be informed of all aspects of municipal activities and to participate more fully in policy development. On the other hand, success of this system requires a high level of input from administrative staff to ensure that council members have the information they need.

Provincial legislation empowers council to adopt by-laws that delegate administrative authority to the various standing committees. Responsibility is exercised through the municipal staff, and the role of each committee is to provide overall policy guidance to staff. Where a chief administrative officer has been appointed, it is *through* this officer that both council and all standing committees relate to other staff. *Special* committees of council are appointed to study or to act in relation to "special" tasks or projects; normally, each special committee is dissolved as soon as it has reported acceptable completion of its assignment.

In practice, municipal administration is shared largely by the chief administrative officer (that is, the city manager, the chief administrative officer, the town clerk, or the municipal clerk) and the committees. The council-committee system has many practical advantages, although too many committees can diminish these advantages and greatly complicate effective administrative decision making.

Summary

Rules of procedure are intended to simplify decision making. In council meetings, it is essential that rules be applied fairly and consistently. This is the primary task of the chairperson, but all members of council should be familiar with the rules so that wrangling about procedure can be avoided.

In Canada, *Bourinot's Rules of Order* has been the standard reference work for legislative bodies. The Kerr and King book, *Procedures for Meetings and Organizations,* incorporates the Bourinot rules, but presents the topic in terms more relevant to present day practices. Each council member should have their own copy. When it is necessary to modify standard rules to accommodate local needs, such local rules should be written down and displayed where each council member has ready access to them.

Rules of procedure spelled out in provincial legislation on municipal organizations take precedence over local rules. These include requirements with respect to voting, attendance, resolutions and by-laws.

In addition to the discussion of various categories of rules, this chapter has dealt with the requirements of various formal documents encountered in municipal council meetings, such as notices of meeting, agendas, and minutes. The place in municipal life of committees, commissions, boards, and other bodies has also been considered.

Chapter X

Offering for Service on Council

Introduction

If you have thought about running for elected municipal office, this book will have introduced you to what local government does and how it is done. This chapter is intended to help you recognize what is involved in becoming a candidate. The first section of this chapter will consider the legal framework for municipal elections and how such elections are conducted. The next section will deal with matters that need to be taken into account when planning and carrying out a campaign.

The chapter speaks particularly to those with little previous election experience, but it may also help those who are seeking re-election. The second time around is often the more difficult campaign to win.

Normally the decision to run for public office is a highly personal one. Few citizens are so universally popular and well-known that droves of people present themselves on their doorstops, urging them to give the community the benefit of their leadership and service. It must be a very pleasant experience for those to whom it happens, but for most candidates the decision to run in an election is reached after personal soul-searching and perhaps consultation with only a spouse or partner and one or two friends. Ultimately, the decision rests with the individual candidate, and it is usually a rather lonely decision.

The Legal Framework

Each province has established its own legal framework for the conduct of municipal elections. Such legislation generally prescribes the timing of elections and the designation of returning officers and their deputies, the requirements for nominations, enumeration lists, polling places, the counting of ballots, and the procedures for recounts. The qualifications to become a candidate are also set out.

Returning Officer

Provincial legislation specifies that where day-long elections are to be held, voting must be conducted under supervision of a returning officer. This is the person who must generally direct and supervise elections for council, with responsibility for the appointment of election officials such as enumerators, revising officers and poll clerks, and for the setting up of polling places required for each polling district. The returning officer must ensure that the election officials are familiar with their duties and that requirements set forth in legislation are followed.

Timing of Elections

The provinces usually require that all municipal elections are held on the same day throughout each province. As a result of amalgamations and major restructuring, there may be temporary exceptions to this rule in some units, but the intent is to require uniformity after the municipal reforms have been completed.

List of Electors

The preparation of an accurate list of electors is the basic step in ensuring that everyone qualified to vote is able to do so. All citizens over the age of eighteen years who have lived in the municipality for a specified time are eligible, with certain exceptions. These exceptions include judges, returning officers, persons committed to certain forms of institutional care, and any person who has been convicted of certain offences such as bribery or fraud within a specified time period.

In 1997, the Federal Elections Commission undertook the establishment of a "permanent" electoral list, with a provision that this list could be made available for provincial and municipal election purposes. Since changes are continually taking place, however, as people move, come of age, acquire citizenship, or die, adequate measures must be taken to ensure that such a list is sufficiently up-to-date for municipal purposes.

However the electoral list is prepared, it will serve three principal purposes:

1. For rulings on qualifications of electors in a process separate from the process of polling.

2. To inform voters before the elections where they have to go to cast their vote.

3. Candidates may use the list as a basis for organizing their electoral campaign.

The preliminary list of electors is required to be posted at accessible locations in advance of elections. A revision process allows for correction of errors or omissions, but all applications must be made in person by the elector or a duly authorized agent. The final list is to be completed by a specified date before the election is to be held.

Eligibility of Candidates

In each province, certain rules govern eligibility for nomination. Generally, a person must meet the qualifications of an elector, although he or she may not need to be resident in the district or ward where the candidate is seeking election. Normally, however, he or she must have resided in the municipality for six months preceding nomination day; must continue to so reside; and must have obtained a certificate that as of nomination day, he or she does not owe municipal rates and taxes. Reasons for disqualification include membership in the House of Commons or Senate in Canada, in the provincial legislative assemblies, or on any other municipal council. Persons employed directly by the municipality or any municipal utility, board or commission are ineligible to run for their own council.

Except in the case of a municipality where council has, through by-law, opted for more stringent regulations, those with a business or contractual relationship with a municipality may still be eligible to seek municipal office. They must, however, if elected, comply with the declaration and withdrawal procedure required by municipal conflict of interest legislation or regulation if they have any interest in a matter being discussed or voted on.

Nomination Procedure

Candidates for the offices of mayor or councillor must be nominated by a specified number of electors who are qualified to vote for the office in the appropriate jurisdiction. Nominations must be submitted in the form required by regulations under legislation, and must be delivered to the returning officer in advance of the election by a specified date. A deposit may be required by the election rules.

As soon as practical after nomination day, the returning officer must ensure that notice of the election is published in a local newspaper, stating the purpose of the election, the names of candidates and the offices they seek, and the date, time, and location of polling places for both the advance poll and ordinary polling.

Polling Places

A "polling district" may be defined as including a ward or a town which is not divided into wards. A "polling division" is one of the parts into which a polling district is divided in order to facilitate the vote. The returning officer has responsibility for setting up the polling divisions, taking into account geographic and population factors.

Advance Polls

Although normally most polling in a municipality takes place on the same day, it is usually required that the returning officer must set up facilities for an advance poll or polls on specified days in advance of the ordinary polling day. The advance poll is for the benefit of those who may be unable to vote on the regular day. These include persons such as the physically handicapped who may find that their regular polling place is inaccessible; anyone scheduled to be in hospital; those objecting for reasons of conscience to Saturday voting; election officials, including agents of candidates; and electors who expect to be at work or away from the municipality on polling day. Votes from the advance poll are counted only after the regular poll has been closed.

Acclamation

Acclamation occurs when the nomination process produces only one candidate for a particular seat. Likewise, where a council is elected "at large", and nominations produce only the number required to fill part or all of the vacant seats, those nominated are elected by acclamation. In such cases, the returning officer notifies the municipal clerk, who at the first meeting of council after the election date must declare the candidates duly elected.

Ballot Papers

Provincial legislation generally prescribes the manner in which the returning officer must keep record of the number of ballot papers distributed to each polling station and how that official must be prepared to provide a detailed accounting of the disposition of each ballot.

Proceedings on Polling Day

Each polling station is under the supervision of a deputy returning officer, who is responsible for blank ballots, ballot boxes, and other supplies required for operation of the poll. The deputy returning officer oversees the proper conduct of balloting, including identification of each elector, handing out of ballots, removal of the counterfoil prior to deposit of each ballot, and at the close of the poll, counting of ballots.

The only persons authorized to be in the polling station include the deputy returning officer, other poll officers, candidates, the returning officer, one agent for each candidate and the candidate's official agent, a peace officer, or any other person necessarily present in order to comply with any section of provincial elections legislation, and, of course during polling, the elector intending to vote. Prior to entering a poll, an agent for a candidate must complete and sign the required form and take the required oath.

Immediately after the close of the poll the deputy returning officer, with the assistance of the poll clerks, must open the ballot box, examine the ballot papers and count the votes. Each person present for the count must have opportunity to examine each ballot and to decide whether it should be counted or rejected. Ballots for the election of a mayor are counted first, followed by the ballots for councillor. A poll statement is completed and a copy distributed on request to each candidate, agent or elector representing a candidate. One copy is inserted in the poll books.

Should the count result in a tie vote, the returning officer must apply to a judge of the County Court or of the Provincial Court for a recount. Should the tie vote be confirmed, the municipal clerk must determine the successful candidate by having a candidate's name drawn by lot.

Recounts

The clerk, if authorized by Council, and any candidate or elector may, within a specified number of days after the polling date, apply for a judicial recount of votes. The application must be filed with the clerk of the court having jurisdiction, accompanied by a deposit as security for costs. After the recount, the judge must certify the result to the municipal clerk, and direct the payment of costs. If, in the opinion of the judge, conduct of the election gave rise to doubts about fairness of procedures, costs may be charged to the municipality, and an order issued to return the deposit to the candidate initiating the recount.

The Election Campaign[1]

The foregoing section outlines the legal framework for municipal elections. A citizen who has decided to run should approach the municipal clerk of the regional, city, town or rural municipality to seek further information or clarification on any particular requirements or procedures that may seem unclear.

The municipal clerk (or the returning officer) will be in a position to provide advice on how, when, and where nomination papers must be filed, and should have information on when the municipal list of electors will be available. In the interval before any new list is prepared, the clerk may be able to provide a list from a previous election, so that candidates can begin work on their campaign at once.

First Steps in Organizing

The size of the district and the number of electors will be important factors in determining the sort of campaign to be conducted. Obviously, the approach to be used in a large city ward with many voters in a compact area will differ widely from what may be needed in large rural district having a few hundred widely scattered voters.

Larger Municipalities

In larger units, the candidate will need to be more highly organized. He or she may need to recruit capable and committed supporters willing to assume specific campaign roles. The key individual in the organization is a general chairperson, someone willing to take overall responsibility in overseeing the efforts of other workers and inspiring them with enthusiasm. This leader should be prepared to replace workers or step in personally in the event the plan shows signs of weakness.

Of similar importance is a finance chairperson who will have control of the campaign budget and finances generally. Depending on the size and nature of the campaign, a publicity chairperson may be required. In less intensive campaigns, publicity may well be handled by the candi-

1 This section of the chapter is based largely on material prepared by Judge Louis E. Moir for the first edition of *A Guide to Local Government in Nova Scotia,* published in Halifax, Nova Scotia, by the Institute of Public Affairs, Dalhousie University, 1977.

date, but consultation with other members of the general campaign committee is essential if feedback is expected.

Other essential roles will likely include a campaign secretary who will keep election materials moving, organize meetings, and ensure efficient communications among workers. A team of captains may be needed to take charge of specific sections of the ward or district. All of these volunteers should place themselves under the direction of the campaign chairperson, with an overall objective of seeing that every voter is contacted at least once.

Only in exceptional circumstances should election workers be paid. If a worker is unemployed, for example, and has contributed a good deal of time to the campaign, the candidate might well consider a reasonable honorarium to be in order. Aside from such unusual circumstances and perhaps in the hiring of a part-time secretary, paid employees should be the exception.

Smaller Municipalities

Less complex are the campaign requirements in smaller towns or rural municipalities, where people generally are easier to know and issues may be fewer. Accordingly, candidates in rural municipal areas usually rely more on their personal campaigns. There may be exceptions, of course, such as when planning or environmental issues give rise to heated debate and elections may bring together competing teams of campaigners with widely differing viewpoints.

In any case, the candidate will wish to tailor his or her approach to the circumstances in the local community. The following suggestions are more applicable when the election is fought on specific issues.

Launching the Campaign

A first question of strategy will be the time and manner chosen to announce an intention to be a candidate. A number of factors will be involved in the decision, including the number of prospective opponents and when these are likely to announce. It is helpful to choose a day and hour when the local news media can make the best use of the announcement so that it will be widely noted by the public. Often the best method is through a small, inexpensive press conference. A written announcement outlining the candidate's platform and reasons for running should be available for distribution to all members of the press and broadcast media.

Deciding the Platform

In the matter of program, the candidate will need to give careful thought, especially if the election is to replace a retiring councillor with a good running record in the district or ward. If there are no apparent major or controversial issues, the candidate should visit a representative number of voters to seek out issues or problems that may be on the minds of residents in the area.

In most cases, however, there will be no lack of major concerns in both the specific and general areas of the ward, district or in the community as a whole. General questions related to ecology, garbage removal, tax rates, buildings, and commercial development usually are of importance to voters in municipal elections. The candidate's position on such issues reveals, at least in part, his or her priority of values. The demonstration of awareness for specific needs of the ward or district is also vital to the campaign, since these matters will represent a considerable part of the successful candidate's responsibility to the area. The major parts of the platform must show whatever plans for the area the candidate honestly believes can be implemented. It is encouraging to note that electorates seem less ready to accept the exaggerated promises that once marked election campaigns.

On the basis of these and other considerations, the candidate should develop a platform, study its implications thoroughly, and then be prepared to promote and defend it publicly. A platform based on sound general principles and human values will not be difficult to defend. It will be important to resist any temptation to jump on a bandwagon because it seems the thing to do. Using prudence and good sense, the candidate should study a particular issue and then come to a conclusion as to what course of action is best for the electoral district and for the entire community.

Once the platform has been defined and developed, the candidate must find effective ways to get it before the public. Before having posters and brochures printed or advertisements prepared for the various media, the candidate will have to consider the costs involved.

Financing the Campaign

In some of the small municipalities where the candidate may know personally almost all the voters, election expenditures may only require at most a few hundred dollars. In other areas, candidates may spend thousands of dollars and then not always with successful results.

There has been recurring debate among provincial political parties on what disclosure should be made on sources of contributions to municipal election campaigns. Unlike the federal and provincial levels, there are currently no legislative requirements for disclosure of how individual election campaigns are financed or how much is spent by municipal candidates. This debate has raised considerable controversy concerning the potential influence over elected officials that may be exercised by persons who have made financial contributions to election campaigns.

Some political leaders suggest that there is no need to fear such pressure unless the candidate is foolish enough to accept a large financial contribution from any one source. Others suggest that confidence of the public in their councillors would be enhanced if the sources of funding were fully and openly disclosed before the election.

Most candidates are probably not able to finance the campaign entirely from their own personal funds and may, therefore, find it necessary to accept financial contributions from supporters. At the outset of the campaign, the candidate must decide if limits are to be placed on contributions from any one individual and whether the names of donors will be made public.

If the campaign is likely to be expensive, the candidate ought to decide how much will be available from personal funds, and then discuss with the campaign finance chairperson the amount of money which might realistically be sought from other sources. The total amount will determine the type of campaign to be conducted. The campaign committee as a whole should be consulted to decide the most efficient use for available funds.

In any event, if it is decided that considerable financial help will be required, the candidate must have a capable finance chairperson who will identify likely contributors, make the necessary approaches and gather in funds, observing the ground rules specified by the candidate.

Personal Contact and Publicity

The spending of money on the campaign is not the primary consideration for success. Some approaches to the public cost little or nothing but are superior to paid advertising in gaining support from voters.

The first and most effective means for gaining public support is for the candidate to meet the voters in person. This can be done in public places such as shopping centres, but is best accomplished by visiting the electors in their offices or homes, taking a few moments to greet the family, indicating willingness to work hard as an elected representative, and answering questions concerning the platform or the election.

The candidate will find it helpful to carry a notebook to record items of particular interest and problems to be dealt with in the municipality. This will serve as a continuous reminder of what electors expect of their representative and what they are hoping can be accomplished in their community. The successful candidate will find that such a record will be invaluable in keeping in touch with citizens and to maintain awareness of their concerns.

In visiting voters, it is seldom wise to ask specifically that the voter support the candidate. It is more effective to request serious consideration for the qualifications and platform of the candidate, in the hope that the voter will reach a favourable conclusion on his or her own.

Where densely populated urban areas are involved, or rural ones many square miles in size, or where the candidate is late in entering a campaign, it will likely be impossible for the candidate to meet every voter personally. The next best thing is for personal supporters to speak to friends and neighbours on a block-by-block basis. This highly valuable contact, which can even be carried out by telephone, is second in importance only to a personal visit from the candidate.

If there are few workers in the campaign who really know the candidate personally, a meeting should be called to allow potential supporters an opportunity to see what kind of person they are being asked to support. Such a meeting should be very informal and unhurried to allow a thorough, open exchange of questions and answers. Only when workers are themselves convinced will they be effective when talking to electors.

Once the door-to-door campaign schedule has been organized, the committee can allocate available funds for posters, brochures, and other advertising. Every printed campaign advertisement of any kind must include the name of the printer and of the person on whose behalf it is being printed.

There are various opinions about the usefulness of posters on lamp posts and fences. Generally this is an acceptable practice only if permission is obtained from the utility company or other private owners. Display of posters on the premises of supporters is one of the least expensive methods of creating public interest and considering the often low election turn out, such stimulation of public attention seems a worthwhile investment.

A campaign publicity chairperson should preferably be someone familiar with both news media and printers. Brochures should be kept simple and to the point, with perhaps one section devoted to the candidate's background and qualifications, and another to the platform. Writing should be in basic but grammatically correct language. Where there are significant numbers of voters with a mother tongue other than

English, the effort should be made to offer written material in the appropriate language.

Depending on funds available, the main brochure should be issued early in the campaign, followed by one or more dealing with issues that arise during the campaign. Mailing costs are high, but if they are to be distributed by volunteers, it is useful to have someone supervise the distribution. Door to door delivery by children may have unfavourable repercussions if the pieces are not properly placed in mailboxes or mail slots.

A good way of delivering literature is for block workers to pass out the copies. The aim should be to use the distribution as a way of contacting the household of everyone on the voting list. Calls could, for example, be assigned to individual block officers, with one captain in charge of about ten block workers. Thus, if there are 3,000 voters, thirty block officers will be needed, each with 100 calls to make, perhaps with a team captain to check that the calls are actually completed.

If the candidate has sufficient workers early in the campaign, most of the doorstep calls can be made prior to the specified revision day. The block officers will then be able pick up errors in the election lists: names which should be added to the lists, and names which should be removed because the voters have moved away, have died or were placed on the lists in error. The procedure is for the block officers to call attention of the revising officer to the required changes, or to advise the individual electors of mistakes that may interfere with their right to vote.

During the time when lists are being revised, another committee should be listing telephone numbers of voters on a master list. This information can be used for a phone canvass, or on election day for calls to urge known supporters to cast their ballots, for offering transportation or babysitting services, or just showing that the candidate is interested in ensuring that voters exercise their right to vote.

Election Day

These preliminary activities aim to gather as many volunteer workers as possible. The candidate will continue efforts to enlist the local press in getting free publicity through announcements, interviews, and public speeches. Finally, election day arrives.

On the big day, the candidate should strive to be seen throughout the community, visiting the polls, greeting people, and generally demonstrating his or her own personal commitment and interest. Note, however, that the candidate must avoid any semblance of insistence in approaching voters at the polls, since many people resent any sense of pressure when casting their votes. Indeed, Section 151 of the Act specifies that the use of intimidation or duress to compel a person to vote is an offence.

At campaign headquarters, the telephone committee will be phoning electors block by block, offering services as previously mentioned. A small transportation committee may be needed to co-ordinate rides to the polls for persons who do not have their own transportation. An important activity will be the door-to-door follow-up by block officers, urging voters to cast their votes before closing time, and talking about their candidate and the work that he or she will be eager to undertake if elected.

Election day is always a long, exciting and physically tiring day. Eventually the polls do close and the ballots are counted. Now the candidate finds out what the democratic process is all about. If you are a winner, be gracious, put aside any animosity which may have developed during the heat of the campaign, and be kind to the defeated candidates. If you are a loser, smile, congratulate the winner, nurse your wounds in private, and be prepared to run another day.

Having Been Elected

The elected representative has, above all, the duty to respect and uphold the democratic system under which we live. It is wise to keep an open mind on every issue, listening to advocates of both sides until the whole question has been properly presented and debated. Only then can the councillor have any clear right to choose one course of action over another.

If, on a specific question, the elected official is the advocate of a particular course of action and forcefully puts forward this point of view, he or she is not released from the obligation to hear other points of view and, if convinced by the opposition, to acknowledge that after all, the original idea may not have been the best solution.

Some observers feel that when elected, councillors should identify with the council as a whole, accepting personal responsibility for decisions reached, even if not personally in agreement with them. Others feel that while the process of government needs a high degree of consensus among members of the municipal council, the individual councillor's own conscience must be obeyed. The councillor must also bear in mind that, while the needs and desires of the constituency must be of particular concern, and while the opinions of citizens must always be seriously considered, in the last analysis the councillor is elected to exercise judgement based on interest in the common good and not necessarily based on popular opinion. The effective representative will recognize that he or she has a duty not only to listen to the citizens, but also to strive to help them to be fully informed about what is "going on".

Summary

We live in a democratic society. We are governed by our peers who are elected by secret ballot. Much can be said about the inefficiencies and errors of this type of system, but it is difficult to think of any other which offers a better possibility for the exercise of freedom. The success of this system of government, or its failure, depends fundamentally on the willingness of persons of good will to serve as elected representatives.

Elections are central to the democratic process. The way they are conducted helps to determine whether government has the confidence of those who are governed. There have been many examples of electoral abuses bringing the whole concept of "politics", government, and even democracy into disrepute. The search for legislative safeguards against such abuses is essential to preserve public confidence in our system. Hence we have election laws and regulations.

With the exception only of persons who are obviously unqualified for some serious reason, everyone who enjoys the liberty of living under the democratic system ought to consider offering his or her name for election to some level of government—probably more than once. Too many people are reluctant to do so or are able to rationalize reasons for not offering to serve.

This chapter has sought to provide a very general outline of the legal framework for the conduct of municipal elections. It has discussed what is involved in service as an elected official, as a way of helping the reader to decide on whether he or she will undertake all that is involved in an election undertaking. Finally, for those who are committed to "taking the plunge", the chapter offers some practical information and advice on the conduct of the campaign.

Very early in the campaign, before the fever and frenzy of the election arouses strong emotions, the candidate ought to resolve, come what may, to say and do nothing which will result in bitterness or hurt feelings for the future. Only thus will confidence in the election process be preserved, and only thus will the successful candidate enjoy the public trust essential for effective service.

Chapter XI

After Thoughts

The search for wisdom will bear fruit only when based on knowledge.

As we stated in the preface to this publication, this book is intended for three different audiences: elected municipal officials who require a primer on local government; appointed municipal officials who require a quick reference; and the general public who seek a broader understanding of what local government is all about. Accordingly, information has been presented in a way that tries to balance the needs of each group without sacrificing relevant content or engaging in unnecessary tedium.

While the information needs of councillors, administrators, and citizens may differ somewhat, there is a more general need to examine some critical perspectives about the nature of local government, its prospects, and its future.

Local government has been and continues to be subject to changes that are largely beyond its own immediate control. These changes involve programs and services, relationships between local and senior governments, how local government is financed and organized, and how it has been affected by the recent trend towards municipal consolidation. What have these changes done to local government? Do they serve to strengthen or weaken local communities? Aside from their ability to deliver local services, does local government continue to serve some wider purpose? What will local government look like in the future? These are important questions that must be asked and that should not be preempted by those who are prepared to make decisions purely on the basis of a "bottom line". To approach answers to these questions, one needs to develop a comprehensive appreciation about the nature of local government. We offer the following as criteria by which to judge the adequacy and effectiveness of any form or variation of municipal government.

Accountability

One of the traditional strengths of local government has been the close relationship that has often existed between its politicians and residents. Where this relationship has been maintained, the local politician may be a neighbour, a school teacher or perhaps the local convenience store operator. It is someone who citizens often know personally or feel connected to because of some shared community experience. Access to one's council member is often only a matter of a short walk, a welcome telephone call or a chance encounter. Absent are the array of formal offices, assistants, and other mechanisms which sometimes serve to juxtaposition themselves between residents and their elected representative. Accordingly, there is more opportunity to interact with the local politician and even to hold him or her accountable.

The size of the ward or district served by individual councillors is an important element in maintaining the type of relationship that leads to effective accountability. In the larger urban areas, some of the sense of neighbourhood may be difficult to maintain. When urban municipalities have increased in size and population, the elected staff, as well as the appointed officials, become more remote and require more layers of management to deal with a wider array of problems. Accountability becomes a more formal process with less interpersonal communication between officials and the public.

Accessibility

Attracting candidates to run for local office is not always an easy task. Too often council seats are filled by acclamation. Without contested elections there is little opportunity for the community to engage in meaningful debate on important public issues. On the other hand, there are important factors which may contribute to a decision to offer for local elective office. What we do know is that willingness to serve on council is rarely motivated by desire for a career change, but rather is an expression of a sincere commitment to the well being of the community. Indeed it is often a logical extension of prior community work.

Larger electoral districts tend to dissuade candidates, particularly those without prior political experience, from offering for office. The cost of the electoral campaign, the additional time commitment, and the general "professionalization" of local politics are often disincentives for community-spirited people. Yet, the democracy process is greatly enhanced when there is a large pool of candidates from which to choose and a resultant elected body that is representative of the diversity which occurs naturally within their community.

Access is a function of the ability of the public to make their views known to their elected representatives. Chapter VI on Public Participation has examined some of the mechanisms and channels that have evolved to maintain communication between citizens and councils. The larger and more complex the municipal unit, the more elaborate may be the procedures required to ensure that such communication links are effective.

Responsiveness

Local government is for local choice. The nature and level of programs and services should reflect, to the degree that is reasonably possible, local preferences and values. Indeed this is, or ought to be, the primary rationale for having a local level government. Inherent in this argument is the notion that some variation between local governments in services and service levels is both desirable and democratic. The alternative is to view local governments as obedient delivery agents for a common set of standardized programs. When this viewpoint predominates, the ability of local government to be responsive to local conditions is compromised.

Experimentation

When local governments are able to shape or adapt programs to meet local needs, there is more opportunity for experimentation. When municipal units are meaningfully involved in program design and delivery, there is likelihood of different and imaginative approaches. Many local governments may develop programs or take approaches that are simple variations of a theme, and the outcome may be problematic. But some will be enormously successful in incorporating a high level of innovation and creativity. Such successes have the potential of providing useful models for other local governments.

In contrast, by their very nature, highly standardized programs provide fewer opportunities for harnessing the knowledge, energy, and creativity of people of commitment at the local level. There is a resultant loss in innovation and learning.

Public Choice

Where we decide to live is a function of many factors. For example, proximity to work is usually important even though lifestyle considerations and modern transportation may reduce the importance of this element. Location decisions are also influenced by factors such as land values, taxation levels, availability of health care facilities, schooling and recreation opportunities, and safety and environmental conditions. In reality, we all have opportunity for some choice as to where we live. Where we ultimately decide to settle will, in the final analysis, reflect what is important and at the same time possible for us. Real differences among municipalities provide for real choices for the public.

The trend of the last three decades to rationalize services in such areas as health care, education, and social welfare has resulted in service consolidation, standardization, and centralization. Often the opportunity costs involve increased travel and longer waiting times. One result has been to make local governments less important factors in our daily lives. We lose our sense of community and make choices out of necessity rather than for aesthetic reasons.

Spread of Power

Changes in provincial-municipal relations have moved in the direction of clearly delineating the respective roles of the two levels. This is often referred to as "disentanglement". The alleged virtues are that by eliminating overlapping responsibilities, greater efficiency will be achieved. It is also argued that there will be greater accountability since there will be no need to share specific service responsibilities between levels of government, and there will also be a clearer demarcation between services to property and services to people.

On the other hand, the involvement of more than one level of government in the delivery of service does have some advantages. The necessity for two levels of government to discuss, consult or even agree with one another as a prerequisite for change provides some safeguards against the unilateral and possible arbitrary use of power by either level.

Democratic Values

Local government is tactile. You can see it in action and it stands in sharp contrast to some of the remoteness and seeming ambiguity and abstraction of senior governments. It is a level of government where individuals can learn about democratic values and readily practice them. Valuing the democratic process, including respect for minority views and recognizing the importance of compromise, is more readily understood and learned at the local level. In other words, local government is well positioned to develop good citizens, a factor that is central to a healthy democracy.

This is being increasingly recognized by the developing world and the emerging democracies. Where mega-projects are being replaced by policies and projects which depend upon and encourage development of representative local governments, the lessons being learned are helping to create more peaceful and flourishing societies.

Summary

In this book we have sought to inform and, at the same time, to provoke discussion about local governmental institutions in the Maritime provinces. We have used a set of criteria that we have found useful in studying and teaching about local government both in traditional academic courses and in lifelong learning programs. While these criteria have not been labelled in the main body of the text, they have been dominant throughout its preparation. In this concluding chapter we offer them as touchstones in considering the future of local government institutions in the Maritime provinces. These are the key issues of *Accountability, Access, Responsiveness, Experimentation, Public Choice, Spread of Power*, and the cultivation of *Democratic Values*.

Even its most optimistic champions must accept that the future of local government is somewhat uncertain. The recent trend towards a standardized, one size fits all form of local government may not portend well for the kind of dynamic and innovative institutions needed to protect and enhance the quality of life in the cities, towns, and rural communities of our region. On the other hand, if enough citizens recognize that local government is for local choice and that variation in the nature and level of service from one local government to another is desirable, there may be continued hope for the future of *Grassroots Democracy*.

Suggested Readings

Dale Richmond and David Siegel (ed.). *Agencies, Boards and Commissions in Canadian Local Government.* Toronto: ICURR Press, 1994.

Michael J. Skelly. *Alternative Service Delivery in Canadian Municipalities.* Toronto: ICURR Press, January 1996.

K. Grant Crawford. *Canadian Municipal Government.* Toronto: University of Toronto Press, 1968.

K.A. Graham and S.D. Phillips (ed.). *Citizen Engagement: Lessons in Participation from Local Government.* Toronto: IPAC, 1998.

Donald J.H. Higgins. *Local and Urban Politics in Canada.* Toronto: Gage Educational Publishing Company, 1986.

John Stewart. *Local Government: The Conditions of Local Choice.* UK: George Allen & Unwin (Publishers) Ltd., 1983.

C. Richard Tindal and Susan Nobes Tindal. *Local Government in Canada, Fourth Edition.* Toronto: McGraw Hill Ryerson Limited, 1995.

Andrew Sancton. *Local Government Reorganization in Canada Since 1975.* Toronto: ICURR Press, 1993.

Allan O'Brien. *Municipal Consolidation in Canada and its Alternatives.* Toronto: ICURR Press, 1993.

Igor Vojnovic. *Municipal Consolidation in the 1990s: An Analysis of Five Canadian Municipalities.* Toronto: ICURR Press, August 1997.

Gerald Hodge. *Planning Canadian Communities: An Introduction to the Principles, Practice, and Participants, Second Edition.* Scarborough: Nelson Canada, 1991.

Report of the Commission on Municipal Reform (Charlottetown and Summerside Areas). Prince Edward Island: Commissioner, December 1993.

Strengthening Municipal Government in New Brunswick's Urban Centres. New Brunswick: Department of Municipalities, Culture and Housing, December 1992.

Task Force on Local Government: Report to the Government of Nova Scotia. Halifax: Department of Municipal Affairs, April 1992.

Richard A. Loreto and Trevor Price (ed.). *Urban Policy Issues: Canadian Perspectives.* Toronto: McClelland & Stewart Inc., 1990.

Richard M. Bird and N. Enid Slack. *Urban Public Finance in Canada, Second Edition.* Toronto: John Wiley & Sons, 1993.

Appendix B

Principal Statutes Relevant to Municipal Government

New Brunswick

Assessment Act
Business Improvement Areas Act
Community Planning Act
Control of Municipalities Act
Elections Act
Emergency Measures Act
Expropriation Act
Fire Prevention Act
Human Rights Act
Municipal Assistance Act
Municipal Capital Borrowing Act
Municipal Debentures Act
Municipal Elections Act
Municipal Heritage Preservation Act
Municipalities Act
New Brunswick Municipal Finance Corporation Act
Police Act
Property Act
Real Property Tax Act
Unsightly Premises Act

Nova Scotia

Assessment Act
Building Code Act
Emergency Measures Act
Environment Act
Fire Prevention Act
Municipal Act

Municipal Affairs Act
Municipal Boundaries and Representations Act
Municipal Conflict of Interest Act
Municipal Elections Act
Municipal Finance Corporation Act
Municipal Grants Act
Municipal Housing Corporations Act
Planning Act
Police Act
Towns Act
Village Service Act

Prince Edward Island

Charlottetown Area Municipalities Act
City of Summerside Act
Emergency Measures Act
Environmental Protection Act
Financial Administration Act
Fire Prevention Act
Human Rights Act
Municipal Boundaries Act
Municipalities Act
Planning Act
Provincial Building Code Act
Real Property Act
Real Property Assessment Act
Real Property Tax Act
Water and Sewerage Act

Index